THE POWER OF
HOPE
FOR CAREGIVERS

HONOR THE RIDE

KAREN SEBASTIAN

**Harris
House
*Publishing***
harrishousepublishing.com

THE POWER OF HOPE FOR CAREGIVERS: Honor the Ride
Copyright © 2018 by Karen Sebastian
Published by Harris House Publishing
www.harrishousepublishing.com
Colleyville, Texas
USA

This title is also available in other formats.

Cover by Christopher Flynn
Cover photo © Matt McK
Author's photo by Sean Sebastian

Internet addresses (websites, etc.) are offered as a resource to you. These are not intended as an endorsement by Harris House Publishing, nor do we vouch for the content of these sites.

Publisher's Cataloging-in-Publication Data

Sebastian, Karen
     The power of hope for caregivers: honor the ride / Sebastian, Karen
        p.cm.
     Includes bibliographical references
     ISBN 978-1-946369-26-0 (pbk.)
     1. Christian Life. 2. Family & Relationships. 3. Eldercare I. Title.
BF575.G7 S43   2017
155.9 37—dc23

Printed in the United States of America.

Hope is a powerful thing, and it is especially powerful when we serve as caregivers for others. In her inspirational and practical book, The Power of Hope for Caregivers, *Karen Sebastian opens up the possibility of hope for everyone who finds themselves in a place of serving their loved ones. Her words bring strength and victory to each reader as she encourages us to honor the ride and embrace the journey.*

KAROL LADD
Bestselling author of *The Power of a Positive Woman*

Karen Sebastian's book, The Power of Hope for Caregivers: Honor the Ride, *is a much needed addition to our lives as caregivers. From her raw and authentic perspective as a caregiver for her own husband, she speaks from a voice of "knowing" and "living" through the waves of joy and grief on a daily basis. Her powerful words and supportive insights feed and nurture our hearts as we walk this challenging, yet honorable road. I have been a caregiver for two elderly parents in our own home until they passed. It is a love journey and having Karen's wisdom and hope for those experiencing the "ride" even more worthwhile.*

LORI DIXON
Visionary Coach, Speaker, Author, TV Personality

Karen Sebastian has been my friend since we were young mothers, and I have witnessed her life as she moved graciously through its many stages. I have known her in the years when she served as the caregiver for aging parents, and then as she cared for her beloved husband, Bill, during his long battle with muscular dystrophy. Karen truly is the woman who can come alongside any caregiver, offering wisdom and advice and even refreshing moments of joyful hope.

MARI HANES
Author and Speaker

Once again, Karen provides practical wisdom and insights that help a caregiver or family member navigate practical and heart challenges in caring for a loved one. The strength of her stories come from one who doesn't speak from a lofty place but rather from having lived in the daily trenches. She will inspire you to do the same. As one of many, I watched her demonstrate dignified care that created a holy culture of honor and hope. May our generation raise the standard for loving care of the most important ones in our lives.

DR. KIM VASTINE
Founder, Ambassador Alliance Int'l
Author and Speaker

Dedication

I dedicate this book to my husband, Rodney, who continually encourages me to stretch further than I think is possible. I treasure our daily time in the Word, physical exercise, and prayer. You are a blessing from the Lord and together we are experiencing the "goodness of the Lord in the land of the living."

Acknowledgements

With hope-filled thanks:

To my Lord and Savior, Jesus, who gives me the strength and wisdom to navigate through many different types of caregiving so I can share this book with you.

To those I had the honor to serve in their time of need. I am grateful for my mother-in-love, Edith Sebastian, who challenged me to become who I am today. My precious Mom, Betty Pritchett, was a prayer warrior until the end and taught me to finish strong. And then, my first husband, Bill Sebastian, showed us all the power of grace under pressure. Dad is still going strong at 101 years of age and demonstrates the right choices of staying active and focusing on ministry because that is who we are.

To my sister, Linda Richey, who is serving as the primary caregiver to Dad. You are practicing honor in a whole new way. I so appreciate you.

To my children, Alanna and Eliberto Rodriguez, Megan and Jacob Scoggins, Sean and Sarah Sebastian for caring for their Dad so faithfully and selflessly. They showed many what excellence in caregiving looks like.

To my grandchildren, Donovan, Devin, Davon, Dominic, Levi, Viola, and Eleanor who inspire me to continue to leave a legacy of honor for future generations. I pray this teaching multiplies favor in all you do and gives you the long life that it promises.

To Harris House Publishing for keeping me on track and bringing out the best in me. Terry, you inspire me to continue to do the hard part so that others can reap the benefit.

Contents

Foreword

by Tracey Mitchell
Speaker • Author • TV Host • CEO

If you are a caregiver, you need hope and strength to face each day. Karen Sebastian's new book, *The Power of Hope for Caregivers*, captures the essence of what it means to find light in a dark season. Having faced the daily challenges of being a caregiver, she learned how to walk thought difficult times with renewed peace and joy.

Recently, my husband suffered a serious injury, leaving him incapacitated for several months. I know first-hand it is hard to see someone you love in pain, especially someone as active as my husband. The first weeks after the accident were extremely stressful as multiple surgeons gave him an unfavorable prognosis. Looking back, I am grateful for the experience that built our faith and gave us the opportunity to reach for miracles. Although my role as my husband's caregiver was shorter than the one you may be fulfilling, I came away with a renewed sensitivity to people fighting for day-to-day courage.

What I appreciate about my friend Karen is her resolve to find hope in dark times. Throughout this book she shares ways to turn tragic times into encouraging encounters. Her real-life examples will inspire you to reach forward in faith and increase your confidence to choose forgiveness over bitterness. She places in your hands tools of hope. Filled with practical application, each chapter empowers you to rise above what threatens to wear you down.

I know God has placed this book in your hands. Karen's quest to discover hope wasn't just for her, but for every person who has or will make a similar journey. Transparent, authentic, and full of wisdom, Karen has a message that will encourage your heart. As you read through each section, allow the words to uplift your spirit and transform your thoughts. Together, let us grow strong in our faith and compassion one for another.

Introduction

May the Eternal repay you for your sacrifices and reward you richly for what you have done. It is under the wings of Israel's God, the Eternal One, that you have sought shelter.
Ruth 12:2 (Voice)

Three women stood huddled against the chill of the morning air and looked at the rapid flow of the river in front of them. They had stopped to gather strength before stepping into the strong current of water in order to cross the Jordan River on their way back to Bethlehem.

"It certainly was a lot easier to cross with Dad and the boys all those years ago," murmured the older woman as she reflected on the memory of her trip from Bethlehem to Moab. "It must have been because of the drought that brought the terrible famine."

Orpah gave her sister-in-law a furtive look as if to say, "Here we go again." She was weary of hearing her mother-in-law, Naomi, repeat the same stories over and over.

"Mom, I love that story of how you all came to Moab. I know you are looking forward to going back to Bethlehem. We are glad we can go with you," Ruth said gently as she hugged the frail frame of her mother-in-law.

Naomi looked up with tears in her eyes. "May God bless you for the way you took care of me and my sons for so many years," she said. "For that very reason I must tell you once again that it is not a good idea for you to travel any further with me. I want you to be happy. You are too young to be burdened with an old, bitter woman like me. Go back home to Moab and live out the rest of your life with your family there. You have a much better chance of finding a husband and having children. This is a bitter pill to swallow. God has dealt me a hard blow."

Naomi had given up all hope for a good future. She saw no way out of her despair and didn't want to drag these young women down with her. She was disappointed with how her life had turned out and put the blame on God with a fatalistic victim mentality that left her desolate and without comfort. Her faith was shaken and she dreaded going back to face the naysayers who had tried to talk her out of leaving Bethlehem during the famine.

While we are not told this specifically, it seems that Naomi's sons were not in good health. I can imagine that Orpah, the one who was married to Chilion (whose name means wasting away and pining), was tired of being the strong one in the relationship. Ruth was married to Mahlon (whose name means sickness or illness), which could have meant that Ruth had already been his care-giver for ten years. These two men died with no children to carry on their name or legacy.

"Listen to what she is saying," Orpah said to Ruth. "It may be best if we just go back home to our families. We don't know anyone in Bethlehem and they may be mean to us. For sure, they are not going to want to marry us since we are from Moab.

"Ruth, come with me," she insisted. "We have to think of our own future. Even Naomi has said that her God has let her down. Let's go back to our old way of living and believing. I am so sick of feeling the weight of caregiving. I don't need this and neither do you."

Naomi nodded in agreement and pushed Ruth toward Orpah, but Ruth refused to leave her and clung to her even more.

The three women hugged each other tightly, sobbing in their shared grief and the ache of broken dreams and expectations. Orpah finally broke away and started walking away slowly, looking back occasionally as if to say to Ruth, "There's still a chance to do the only thing that's best for your future."

"Are you sure about this?" Naomi asked Ruth. "I set you free from all promises to care for me so you can go catch up with her. She has gone back to her family and to her gods."

"Mom, stop asking me to leave you! Stop pushing me away, insisting that I stop following you! Wherever you go, I will go. Wherever you live, I will live. Your people will be my people. Your God will be my God. Wherever you die, I will also die and be buried there near you. May the Eternal One punish me — and even more so — if anything besides death comes between us," replied Ruth adamantly (Ruth 1:16-17 Voice).

They stood there, staring into the distance until Orpah's silhouette disappeared on the horizon. They slowly turned around and stepped into the flowing water to cross the Jordan River. Each time that Naomi would stumble, Ruth would help her. They somehow made it across the treacherous waters and continued on their journey to Bethlehem.

This is how I imagine the details of the story of Ruth in the Bible. It reads like a rags-to-riches romance novel with a main protagonist who was an unlikely heroine with a shady past. There are few details given, yet many clues that give us insight into what motivated this powerful hope ambassador. We have the benefit of knowing as we read it that it has a wonderful ending. At this point in her life however, in order to care for Naomi, Ruth was essentially giving up her future happiness and the prospect of finding a husband and giving birth to her own children. Even after caring for an invalid husband for ten years, she was willing to rewrite the final chapters of her mother-in-law's life through powerful hope and honor. Ruth embraced honor with obedience to God and devoted her life to serving willingly and lovingly. In turn, her heart of service and hard work opened the way to unprecedented favor and carried her to a great future.

Ruth's decision to honor her mother-in-law earned her a spot in the Bible and a place in the lineage of the Messiah. We will explore more details of the special relationship between these two amazing women in later chapters. Suffice it to say that here Ruth's future was uncertain, yet she knew that she was headed in the right direction with renewed hope and purpose.

You probably picked up this book because you are facing difficulties in a caregiving scenario or know someone who needs a healthy dose of hope in this challenging role. It's not easy to add on the responsibilities of caring for the needs of others when you already feel overwhelmed. You may resent the situation and feel like you have no choice in the matter. There are honor keys throughout the book to remind you to embrace honor, for it will increase the opportunities of enjoying the ride of your life while leaving a legacy of love and extending your life. Each chapter ends with a scripturally based prayer that can steady you when you feel like you are going under.

My experience as a caregiver spans over three decades in four distinct scenarios. I know from personal experience how demanding this role becomes and how taxing it can be physically, emotionally, and spiritually. I wish I could say that I've always felt hope and honored the gift set before me. Still, I am grateful for each situation and, if I had to do it all over again, I would jump right in. The only difference is that now I would be sure to put on my life jacket and would position myself for the ride of my life. I want to share practical tips on handling the details, becoming an advocate, getting others to help, taking care of yourself, and empowering your loved one to finish strong. All this can all be done with hope and honor out of obedience to the Lord.

I so wish I could sit down with a cup a coffee (or tea) and hear the details of your unique story. I share mine with the prayer that it inspires hope and awakens the possibilities of adding honor to the caregiving atmosphere. You can get through this difficult season with dignity and strength. You will one day look back on these hectic days with fond memories of having done what only you could do. You can rewrite the closing chapters in the lives of those you love by helping them to finish strong while investing in treasured memories for future generations, just like Ruth did.

HONOR THE RIDE

~ 20 ~

Gaining Perspective

I grabbed a pillow off the couch and ran out to the back yard. I felt I had nowhere else to go to escape. I didn't want my little ones to see me display this level of frustration. I screamed into the pillow, "I hate this! I hate this!" I felt alone and defeated as I gave vent to my anger. I felt like I was stuck in a deep canyon going down treacherous rapids that no one had trained me to navigate. My emotions were like a raging river that threatened to drown me; yet somehow, I always managed to come up for air.

We had just moved in with my mother-in-law after my father-in-law died. She seemed seriously depressed and refused to eat. With a five-year-old and a toddler in tow, we packed up and moved into her house. It felt like I had no choice but to jump on board the white-water raft and head down the river. The worst part is that I felt like I had no paddle to guide the vessel and no life jacket when I fell off.

My husband was busy with the responsibilities of pastoring a thriving church. On the personal side, he was worried and weary. On top of grieving his father's death, he was now convinced that his mother would die if we were not there for her. I hesitated to burden him with my feelings and concerns. I was trapped in a cycle of anger, guilt, and sorrow. I needed a change in perspective in order to see my life circumstances in a different light.

I didn't ask for this role of caregiver. It fell to me by default somewhat like the line of potential volunteers where everyone else simultaneously steps back, leaving you standing there as the one who appears to have taken a step forward.

It can seem like no one else sees all you do. You may feel unappreciated, frustrated, angry, or having no voice. I did. All I knew to do was complain about it, which only made me feel worse. I forgot that I had the choice to choose my perspective. That's the reason that I have chosen the white-water rafting as an analogy for the ride of a caregiver. For the sake of this analogy of a powerful caregiving model, the raft is hope and the paddle represents honor. There are those times when the waters seem smooth and manageable. Then suddenly, you hear the roar of the upcoming rapids. There is no way to get out of the water, so you make a run for it. As you just let loose and 'go for it,' it can become an exhilarating experience.

CHOOSING HOPE

Think of the last time you used the word hope in a conversation. Most people use it the following way: "I sure hope this caregiving situation works out. There are so many bad memories and hurts from the past that I hope I can overlook. I sure hope I can make it." In this context, the word hope loses its true meaning. It doesn't help matters when everyone chimes in with their bad experiences in similar circumstances. Even though they are sad, like Orpah, they turn away from the fear of the unknown and always wonder what could have been. (Read the introduction to get more details on the story of Ruth and Naomi, or read the first chapter of Ruth in the Bible).

In the Bible, there are several different words that are translated as hope. One such word is the Hebrew word *tisqvah* that literally means a cord that carries you forward with a sense of expectancy and trust in the Lord. You feel confident everything will work out even if you may have to wait for a season. It is the word used in one of my favorite verses: "For I know the plans I have for you," says the Lord, "plans for good and not for evil, to give you a hope and a future" (Jeremiah 29:11). No matter what you are experiencing as a caregiver, there is a good future in the days ahead. You can hang on to the cord of hope and look forward with confident expectation that you will come out on the other side of the experience with greater confidence, understanding, and wisdom.

As you prepare to go through the white-water rapids, it's important to get on the raft of hope with the confidence that you are going to make it through. Also, it's important to gain skills in using the paddle to move forward and around the rocks. There really is no going back and as you trust God, you are able to acquire the skills you need right when you need them. Your confidence will grow with every challenge as you faithfully do the next thing that is set in front of you.

COMMITTING TO HONOR

You need to use a paddle to guide the raft through choppy waters. For the sake of our analogy, we are going to consider honor to be that paddle. Honor makes a huge difference in caregiving. The fifth commandment given by God to Israel through Moses has a promise attached to it. In Exodus 20:12 it says, "Honor your father and your mother that your days may be long upon the land which the Lord your God is giving you." Deuteronomy 5:16 takes the promise one step further by including the promise of favor in your life when you choose to honor your parents. This is a foundational principle that all caregivers should remember and celebrate even while navigating through difficult times.

The Hebrew word that expresses honor in these two verses is *kabed*. It has opposite meanings. On the negative side, kabed can be heavy, burdensome, dull, or severe. Meanwhile on the positive side, it means filled with glory, weighty, noble, or wealthy. I have experienced both sides of the word and am grateful to have risen above the weight of obligation to the joy of serving and honoring fully. The rewards of exploring the positive version of honor are priceless and long-reaching. For this reason, you will find Honor Keys at the end of each chapter of the book to inspire you to embrace the noble side of loving service to someone you love who is in great need.

We live in a society that seems to have forgotten the true meaning of respect and favorable regard. Many parents go through tremendous difficulties as they perpetuate the abuse or neglect they suffered in their own childhood. In these situations, the communication breaks down over the years as family members separate and alienate themselves from those who have wronged them. Honor does not condone this behavior; instead, the essence of honor is to recognize the role of a person in your life and trust God in their execution of that appointment. Parents may fail in many ways and hurt their children. While this is not right or in God's plan, when it's your turn to take care of them in their final days, you have an opportunity to change the legacy and direction of your family, live a longer life, and experience unprecedented favor in all you do. You have been given the chance to rewrite the end of the story and redeem the pain by creating powerful positive memories to take the place of the painful ones. The redemptive quality of honor is applicable to much more than just parent-child relationships. In any type of caregiving situation, honoring the one you care for will empower you with the peace of mind that comes with no regrets.

FINDING TRUE MOTIVATION

In our independent world, obedience seems like a harsh word and one that we do not like. However, to survive in caregiving, we must find the proper motivation to align our efforts for others with obeying God. You may have heard the verse that says, "Obedience is better than sacrifice" (1 Samuel 15:22).

Are you a martyr? I certainly was. Are you complaining about how no one is helping you? Part of my difficulties came from a sense of unfairness and self-pity. When I did finally say something, I was angry and accusatory. This caused those who could have helped me to put up their defenses. I clammed up and became even angrier with the situation. As I mentioned earlier, I also spent a lot of time complaining, thus hoping that others would jump in to assist me. Instead, they felt sorry for me and commiserated with me, yet did nothing because I was only hinting at what I needed. Today, I would speak up and ask specifically for help in areas of need.

Focus on being obedient to do what only you can do for a short season that will never be duplicated. Right now, it seems hard, yet one day in the future you will look back and will be amazed at what you were able to do. At the end of an exhausting day, you can rest knowing that the Lord is pleased with what you have done for someone else.

CHRONIC CAREGIVER

My first caregiving season started years ago, after my father-in-law died and we moved in with my mother-in-law who was struggling with a deep depression. It was one of the hardest times of my life as she was very angry with God and her situation in life. At that point, I will confess that I did not always respond correctly. In fact, often I reacted harshly and made matters worse. I tried to honor her because she was my husband's mother, yet complained to those closest to me about her behavior. There were subtle ways in which others affirmed my position and even laughed sarcastically with me. Be honest! How many mother-in-law jokes have you heard? I have found it very difficult to write about this because of the latent anger it has stirred up even now and my deep sense of regret for not having honored more fully. I don't want you to have to experience that in your life.

The challenge with caring for someone with a chronic condition is that the scope increases gradually and can sneak up on you. In most cases, when you are the caregiver for someone who is aging, the level of support increases with each passing year. It may start as a need to help around the house or to pay the bills. It often gradually becomes worse and it leaves you wondering what you need to do and how long the caregiving assignment will last. It's the very uncertain nature of this assignment that makes it challenging.

LONG DISTANCE CAREGIVER

My second caregiving role featured my mom, who was thousands of miles away. I had no way of suspecting that she was beginning to suffer signs of dementia until visiting their home. My heart broke to walk into a smelly, dirty house and to see the stains on Mom's housecoat. I was surprised and shocked because she sounded great on the phone. My parents kept saying everything was fine when clearly it was not. Dad covered for Mom and never fully acknowledged that there was anything wrong with her. My sister and I tried to coax them to move closer to one of us, but they were determined to keep their independence and stay in their home. I felt guilty for being a bad daughter and was caught in a conundrum of not being able to leave the daily responsibilities of my life in another state to care for them. My siblings and I went to visit every chance we got and prayed for the best as things deteriorated. How do you know if you're doing the right thing or if you are doing enough?

One of the biggest challenges in a long distance caregiving relationship is knowing what to believe when your gut tells you something is just not right. Another difficulty is knowing the timing on when to insist that your loved one(s) move closer to family. You want them to have their independence and live a full life, yet it can be harder for them to be so far away when you suspect all is not well. The greatest piece of advice is to stay in touch consistently and find someone who is local to be your eyes and ears.

ACUTE CAREGIVER

My first husband, Bill, lived his entire life with Muscular Dystrophy. We didn't receive the official diagnosis until twelve years before his death. He was very self-sufficient until the last two and a half years, when the disease progressed rapidly and affected his body's core. An extended hospital stay left him requiring full attention and care. He ended up needing a full-time ventilator for breathing and using a suction machine for his saliva. I fed him through a feeding tube (g-peg) and monitored him carefully. The challenge with this caregiver position was doing things that I had always avoided that involved body fluids and medical procedures. I learned quickly and did the best that I could with what we had to work with. Through it all, his attitude was amazing, yet the full-time care took its toll physically and emotionally.

This caregiving position is a difficult one that more and more people are filling after an emergency situation when a loved one comes home and requires constant care. Many times, our aging parents have a very limited time in a rehabilitation facility and no long-term care insurance. There are many sacrifices being made in many families as one of them gives up their work to care for their elders. It can often involve a lengthy recovery time and a great deal of adjustment for all involved.

HONORING CAREGIVER

Over the years, I have learned honoring principles that I have been eager to apply to caring for my father. I recently chose to spend a month with Dad so he could decide if it was time for him to move in with my sister and her family. We are applying these principles in our current caregiving for him and it is making a huge difference in all our lives. I'm grateful for the chance to improve in this area and to share the joy of that experience as well. It's a priceless opportunity to see these principles in action as we incorporate more people into the honoring experience and celebrate the life of a truly remarkable man.

As I reflect on the caregiving scenarios of the past, there were cloudy days and turbulent waters. I am grateful for the honor that I was able to integrate into the latter years of my caregiving ride. I want to sit beside you as you navigate the situations where you just want to give up. My prayer is that this book will infuse you with a healthy dose of hope and hand you a life jacket and a paddle that you can use to keep going even when you get knocked into the turbulent water. I pray my candor will be a blessing and a relief as you realize you are not alone.

In the challenges of caregiving, recognize that you can choose hope and honor when you obey what God wants you to do no matter what others do or have done. These principles change the atmosphere and establish a legacy within your family. In fact, honoring those who might not have honored you is a powerful release to longevity and favor. The challenge truly lies in reflecting on what is happening in the moment and celebrating every twist and turn as you continue to ride the rapids with confidence knowing that calm waters are ahead. You will one day look back on this season, as I have in this book, and marvel at the consistency of hope rays that appear as you go through dark times.

Hope Tools

CHOOSE TO BE A HOPE AMBASSADOR

A Hope Ambassador is someone who assesses the level of difficulty in the white-water rapids ahead and makes sure that everyone has the right equipment and training to get through it. They bring a sense of peace and confidence to tough times as they look ahead. They are the one who picks a lens of hope, rather than defaulting to complaints and martyrdom. Have you ever thought about the fact that you are right where you need to be in caregiving so that you can share hope? If so, then become a Hope Ambassador who acknowledges difficulties, yet knows that God has a plan for it all. He is working in the midst of the stress to make you stronger and to show His love through every twist and turn of this ride. You honor God when you honor those who are in need. As you love them, you are loving Jesus. He is shaping and molding your life to become all that He has destined you both to be.

CHOOSE TO LEARN

I remember how overwhelmed I was when Bill came home from the hospital with a feeding tube. I was afraid I would make a mistake that would make the situation worse. The great part is that I was able to master the techniques and gradually become comfortable with what needed to be done. These caregiving experiences will teach you that you are stronger than you think. The terminology that seems like a foreign language now will soon become familiar. You will be able to ask the right questions at the right time. You will be able to provide for an urgent need and have the joy of making a difference. Write down what you are learning while it is still new and fresh. In that way, you can invite others to come along for the ride.

CHOOSE TO LAUGH

Looking back on this dark season of my life, I realize now that I had stopped laughing. I was so angry that I walked around with a heavy heart and a scowl on my face. I now know that I can always choose to find the humor in everything that happens to me as there are so many things that can bring joy. It becomes a very personal decision to create an atmosphere where it is okay to have fun even in the midst of the mess. Make a commitment to seek the humor in everything you do. Learn to laugh at yourself, especially if you land in the water. I know it's hard sometimes, but a good laugh benefits you physically, emotionally, and spiritually.

Honor Key

Honor the one you care for because of who they are (not what they do or have done), and trust God to work out the details.

Prayer

As I begin my ride as a caregiver, I want to acknowledge Your love and grace that fill me with hope through the unexpected parts of my ride. I have so much to learn, yet I know that I will have everything that I need as I devote myself to doing what is good in order to provide for the urgent needs of _____ (name of care recipient). I find great joy in being productive and making a difference (Titus 3:14).

I am thankful that I have the privilege of being a Hope Ambassador in the dark places where the need for You is so great. My prayer is that all who see my interaction with _____ (name of care recipient) will grow in their respect for You and give You glory. I am thankful that You are sending the flooding waters to move me forward and destroy all the lies of the enemy (Isaiah 59:19 Voice). I will no longer feel overwhelmed or fearful if my raft tips over. I will hold my breath, keep paddling, and trust that You will rescue me and draw me out of deep waters. I know You are mindful of all that concerns me because You delight in me (Psalm 18:17-19 NLT).

I choose today to learn all I can and to, above all, hold on to honor and seek to obey You in every detail. I will hold on to hope even when I get knocked into turbulent waters (Proverbs 4:13 NLT). I rejoice in all that You are doing in this season and find humor in everything that we go through. I will continually declare Your greatness and goodness in the midst of the torrential waters (Psalm 70:4). In Jesus's name. Amen.

Hope Expressions

The proof that we love God comes when we keep his commandments and they are not at all troublesome.
1 John 5:3 (MSG)

Why me?

As cited in caregiver.org, the American Association of Retired Persons conducted recent studies to determine what the average caregiver looks like.

- Average age: 49
- Gender: 60% are Female
- Employment: Fulltime
- Average time caregiving per week: 20 hours
- Average span of care: Five (5) years
- Other factors: One third have children and grandchildren

The problem with statistics is that they don't tell the whole story. For many, the caregiving responsibilities are added to a full-time job and other responsibilities at home with children and grandchildren. The statistics don't show the great personal sacrifices and adjustments you had to make as you assumed a role you never really chose in the first place. There are countless hours of thankless work, worries about finances, and crash courses on medical procedures that stretch you beyond what you ever thought possible. You learn to be an advocate for your loved one which requires the balance of practical knowledge along with the skill of a seasoned negotiator to find the right balance between the person's wishes (or stubbornness) and the doctor's orders.

One of the hardest parts of becoming a caregiver is that most people enter the role without any preparation or proper training. Once you are there, you often feel isolated and alone without knowing who to go to for help and guidance. For many, the financial sacrifice becomes an ongoing challenge as you cut back on your hours or quit your job, thus losing not only the current income, but future retirement benefits.

Each caregiving scenario is unique and challenging. It is exhausting and exhilarating. It can feel unfair and, at the same time, it can be an adventure you are thankful you did not miss. You could say that it is a little like white-water rafting. You went for a short ride down the river and started out slowly. At some point, however, the process accelerated and you were hit by unexpected waves amid the rocks and rapids. You find yourself consumed with decisions and responsibilities that threaten to overwhelm you. Just when you think you have a handle on it, a simple call can send you cascading down another set of rapids with a brand-new set of priorities.

The good news is you can hope for more than merely surviving this season. It is possible to thrive amid the chaos of caregiving. While it can seem like it will never end, I am here to tell you that it does end, and when it does, it's sad.

Preserving Dignity

The details of my late husband's last doctor's appointment are indelibly engraved in my memory. It was a routine visit with the pulmonologist to check Bill's oxygen levels. In our past appointments, this doctor had been pleased that Bill's lungs were still strong even though his diaphragm no longer functioned. The full-time ventilator pushed the air in and out of his lungs via a c-Pap mask over his face.

"Mr. Sebastian, I must insist that you get a tracheostomy," the doctor said grimly.

With no hesitation, Bill signed N – O, and then very deliberately grabbed his marker and wrote, "NO." It was the size of the entire white board we had taken in so that he could communicate with the medical staff.

"I respect that, Mr. Sebastian," acknowledged the doctor. "I just want you to know that as your doctor it is my duty to let you know the risk you take by not having this procedure done."

"Wait just a minute, honey," I said quickly. "Hear out what the doctor is telling us."

The doctor went on to explain that because of the lack of muscle tone in his face due to the type of Muscular Dystrophy and the continual flow of air through the mask, it was more and more difficult for the oxygen levels to stay at optimum levels.

I don't remember much else about that doctor's appointment. I felt angry and frustrated. Once we were situated back in the car and on the road home, I turned to him and asked angrily, "Why won't you follow the doctor's orders?" I glanced over briefly as he began answering me with sign language. I kept sneaking glances over at him while I merged on to the road to take us home. Finally, I blurted out, "Are you saying that you're HELD? What are you talking about?" I snapped.

He just looked at me and kept signing. His white-board was in the back seat so I couldn't reach it without pulling the car over.

"We can talk about it more when we get home and I can get your whiteboard," I said angrily.

I was fuming inside. I had barely managed to get him in to the car. He was getting worse and there was nothing I could do about that. My internal dialogue was not good as I thought, *What good does it do us to have the best medical team in the world if Bill is just going to be stubborn about it all and not do what the doctors want him to do?*

Over the years that I had served as my husband's caregiver, I discovered there were areas where he would not give one single inch. It looked like this was one of those areas. Once we got home and Bill was seated in his chair, I asked him again, "Why, won't you follow the doctor's orders?" This time he wrote on his whiteboard "I'm healed."

Tears filled my eyes as I realized that this was not just stubbornness – this was an act of faith. As his caregiver, I gave him the dignity and honor of making this important decision.

The next Monday night, one of the most difficult, yet rewarding, caregiving assignments in my life ended when my husband died during the night. I am grateful that I had the opportunity to care for him with hope and honor his wishes.

I will never know what a different direction our lives could have taken if I had not respected Bill's strong desire to wait for the healing of the Lord, nor do I want to second-guess it. Ultimately, he was healed and is now in a perfect body in the presence of his Savior and Lord. He is raising his arms completely, running around Heaven, and worshipping his Savior at the top of his lungs.

Bill's official medical diagnosis was Facioscapular-humeral Dystrophy, which is the long name for an adult-onset form of Muscular Dystrophy referred to as FSHD. It usually is a slow-moving disease where the muscles deteriorate gradually and the one afflicted with it may simply associate the symptoms with growing older. During the last two and a half years of his life here on earth, he required more and more care.

When I took my vows on our wedding day, I said, "In sickness and in health," never imagining the course our lives would take or the treacherous waters we would have to navigate. Looking back on it now, I wouldn't trade one minute of it. Extending respect and honor changed the dynamic of our lives. It was how we lived before the health issues escalated and allowed us to apply these principles during difficult times. We discovered hope and courage in the toughest turns of the journey. Honor became a part of our lives as we incorporated it into our family's culture and reflected these principles in the way we spoke to each other. We continued to laugh at the weirdest things and enjoyed being together. The entire family rallied around my husband, and we celebrated everything together. They took turns taking care of him and creating strong memories. In the end, he still could call the shots as to what he wanted to do. I am grateful that I honored his choices. I am thankful we have no regrets.

Somewhere during this ride over rough water, we learned to tap into a deep reservoir of hope that sustained us as we adjusted and kept living and loving. There were many times I just wanted to give up as I navigated the unknown waters of medical procedures, insurance claims, handling body fluids, applying medicine to infected bed sores, preparing the food for the feeding tube, etc. I was blessed because my husband was gracious and kind through it all. He had a special grace that allowed him to fully express his gratitude and find a sense of humor in it all. Not everyone has that same blessing.

CAREGIVERS NEED HONOR

Caregiving is a hard and often thankless job. It comes with many responsibilities and what feels like a never-ending list of things to do on top of all your other duties. Here's a word of advice – serve as a caregiver with honor and hope. Give freely expecting nothing in return. Protect your heart against bitterness and resentment because these negative emotions will deplete your energy supply.

How can you neutralize such strong emotions? Grab on to the promises that honor brings by choosing your perspective. Honor means far more than merely going through the motions. It involves the deepest expressions of respect, admiration, appreciation, consideration, love, dignity, and affection. Honor requires the action of positive expressions to help someone, bring joy, and improve the quality of their life. Caregiving often takes on even greater weight because it has the element of providing protection and care when they can no longer take care of themselves.

CAREGIVERS NEED PRAYER

The caregiving journey may feel like an unpredictable ride through a deep canyon where the only way out is to keep riding down the river even though there are rapids ahead. You are not alone in feeling that way. Seven in ten caregivers (73%) say praying helps them cope with caregiving stress.

An inexperienced person would be crazy to venture out alone down the river. You need an experienced guide who can chart the best course for your level of experience and the ever-changing weather. It is comforting to know that our Lord Jesus was a caregiver during his life on this earth. As the oldest son in a Jewish family, he was responsible to care for his mother after the death of his adopted father, Joseph. Scholars generally agree on this fact because there is no mention of Joseph during the ministry of Jesus. Besides, when Jesus was dying on the cross he turns to John the Beloved and asks him to care for His mother, Mary. The Lord fully understands the exhaustion you feel and knows how to help you where you need it most. In Hebrews 4:15-16 (MSG) we read:

"He's been through weakness and testing, experienced it all—all but the sin. So, let's walk right up to Him and get what He is so ready to give. Take the mercy, accept the help."

Prayer opens your heart to the possibilities of the future and protects your heart from deep wounding. Prayer empowers you to release your burdens to the One who understands so He can carry them. You are no longer alone. You are no longer a victim. You have incredible opportunities to embrace hope and spread it to others.

CAREGIVERS NEED HOPE

You have a big heart and care deeply for your loved ones who need you. You also may be in a situation where you desperately need help and appreciation. You may have never planned for your life to turn out this way. In fact, you probably pushed the thought far from your mind. It can seem that others are enjoying themselves far more than you are. They pick up and go whenever they need to while you are stuck doing the dirty jobs.

Your role as a caregiver may have begun abruptly after an emergency fall or simply realizing that your parents needed more help. The challenge came when you added all the extra demands to an already busy life. You may have instantly become part of what is known as the "sandwich generation" as you still have children at home while caring for your aging parents. The common feeling is one of being overwhelmed. You may be instantly expected to perform medical procedures and take care of areas that you thought you would never be able to do. No matter where you find yourself in your caregiving journey, remember it is more than a quick ride down some rapids. You are in this for the long haul. Ask for help. Rely on the wisdom of others who have been through similar experiences before you. Most of all, rely on the hope that only the Lord can give you every time it seems like you are going to capsize. You will gain strength and wisdom as you go and even unveil new levels of blessings in this journey as you come to the other side of the experience.

There are clear warnings about neglecting what matters most — you! In taking care of others, you can continually give up what's most important. It starts with one decision to stay home when others go out because it's easier than finding someone to care for your loved one. Taking the path of least resistance can then become a pattern that compounds into an unhealthy state of mind. Here are some Hope Tools that will help break that pattern and put you back on a road of health and balance during this difficult time.

Hope Tools

GIVE FREELY

You are on your caregiving journey whether you want to be or not. It may be a short ride or it may stretch out into years. Either way it is hard. The good news is that you get to choose your perspective. Every day you get to choose your attitude and the approach you will take in response to what happens. Is it the end of the world or is it an adventure in patience, love, and grace? If you have had a stormy relationship in the past, you get to rewrite the end of the story. When it is all over, will you look back and see opportunities that you have missed? Don't miss them by harboring resentment and anger that deplete your energy supply.

Negativity and complaining siphon off your stamina and vitality. Instead, choose to honor the one you care for by giving your time freely and determining to make it a fun ride. Make the time together memorable by asking questions and listening intently for memories. Take a video so you can share with future generations. Many times, the final days can become precious as your loved one opens up in new ways to reveal secrets and forgotten memories.

Choose a Positive Outlook

Choosing a positive attitude can be extremely difficult when there are health challenges because health care professionals are committed to being honest and frank about what they see. It doesn't mean that they don't believe that miracles happen because I am sure they see them. However, they will lay out the worst-case scenario from a factual and scientific viewpoint. It is important to find a balance between following doctors' orders, taking medications, and believing God for healing.

A hope perspective does not mean that you deny the seriousness of what you are facing. Instead, it will allow you to interpret what is going on in an informative way rather than taking a pessimistic approach. Ask the difficult questions and learn all you can about the situation. When you believe that God has a purpose and plan for every situation in your life and the lives of those you love, you will remain peaceful and will find joy in the midst of the struggles. Choose to look through the lens of hope because it's powerful!

HONOR KEY

Encourage the health care professionals to speak directly to the patient and listen carefully so you can empower the patient in his/her decisions.

PRAYER

Thank you Lord for the privilege of caring for _____ (name of care recipient). Grant me the strength and courage to face the overwhelming and daunting tasks set before me as we face _____ (name of illness or condition). I trust You to make me powerful and to give me favor as I talk to doctors and facility directors. Thank You that I can be loving and firm with them and with my loved one(s) (2 Timothy 1:7). Thank You for the discipline that I can develop in this season. Thank You that I have everything that I need right now and that this season will not last forever. Thank You for the gift of hope and laughter as I honor the one(s) I serve.

I am thankful that when life is dark, your light shines into the darkness (John 1:5). I ask you to flood my heart with your mercy and compassion. I want to share freely, expecting nothing in return. I thank You that I do not need to be afraid when the news is bad because I put my trust in You. I thank You that my heart can be confident and completely free from all fear (Hebrews 12:12). I receive strength and power from You in the midst of these circumstances. Thank You that, as I choose to give honor freely, You will provide the strength and power that I need to thrive in my season as a caregiver. You become strong in me when I am at my weakest point (2 Corinthians 12:10 Voice).

In Jesus's name. Amen.

Hope Expressions

They share freely and give generously to those in need. Their good deeds will be remembered forever. They will have influence and honor.
Psalm 112:9 (NLT)

Honoring Your Role as a Caregiver

The two forlorn women formed a bittersweet picture as they slowly shuffled along the dusty road. Their coarse garments made from burlap were covered with dust that went everywhere as the younger of the two readjusted the older woman's shawl in a feeble attempt to shield the older lady from the burning sun. They had been traveling for days and were exhausted.

"Just leave me here to die," Naomi gasped as she coughed. "I really don't think that I have the strength to go on."

"Mom, we can do this," Ruth said gently to the older woman. "We don't have that much more to go and you have people who care about you in Bethlehem. They will be happy to see you."

"I don't know about that. I do know that my friends will be surprised to see me bringing back a Moabite woman like you," she replied bitterly.

Ruth felt a twinge of apprehension as she tried to picture the reception she would receive. For a fleeting moment, she wondered if she should have left with her sister-in-law Orpah. As a Moabite, not only was she a foreigner, but there was also the shame associated with her family's past. Seven generations earlier, after the destruction of Sodom and Gomorrah, Lot's daughters got him drunk and became pregnant by him. Ruth was facing the possibilities of never remarrying or having children. Hope grew inside her as she remembered the promise in her declaration that she would take care of Naomi with God's help. She hugged the frail woman a little tighter and said, "Let's keep going, Mom. We can do this."

The two women created quite a buzz when they finally arrived in Bethlehem. Friends came out to greet their old friend Naomi, who had left years before, and were shocked when they saw her. She was stooped with sorrow and seemed devoid of hope. She started telling them all about the troubles they had encountered in the land of Moab. At the end of her monologue, she looked up with tears in her eyes and said, "Stop calling me Naomi (pleasant)."

"What do you want us to call you now?" they asked.

"Call me Bitter. The Strong One has dealt me a bitter blow. I left here full of life, and God has brought me back with nothing but the clothes on my back. Why would you call me Naomi? God certainly doesn't. The Strong One ruined me," she replied as she began to weep (Ruth 1:20-21 MSG).

They looked away without knowing what to say as Ruth went to help Naomi up so they could go to their humble home.

"Mom, I know you feel that way right now, but remember how you thought you would never be able to make the long walk from Moab? God will give us both strength for the days ahead. I am going to need your wisdom and strength because this is all new to me," Ruth said gently.

HONOR BEFORE FAVOR

Many of us would have done exactly what Orpah did when given the opportunity. She left when Noami tried to push her away. Who wants to attach themselves to a negative and bitter person? She may have already had to take care of a declining husband who did not meet her personal needs for affection and fulfillment. It is fascinating that there is no further mention of Orpah in the Bible. Jewish tradition says that Orpah was rejected by her family in Moab and ended up with the Philistines where she gave birth to giants. One of these giants was named Goliath, who fought and lost to David, Ruth's grandson. By turning away from the opportunity to honor her mother-in-law, she also gave up her relationship with the God of Israel and faced more disappointment.

Ruth, on the other hand, declares that Naomi's God will be her God. Ruth honored with no strings attached and gave up control of her own future knowing that it could be difficult and lonely. The most amazing part of this story lies in what happens when Ruth follows through with her part of the commitment.

When the dust settled once they arrived in Bethlehem, it was time for Ruth to go to work. Fortunately, it was harvest season. Favor started to manifest when Ruth stopped at the field of Boaz who was a relative of her late husband. She followed Naomi's advice implicitly and was the channel of great blessing to her mother-in-law. Through a law that required a relative to marry the widow, Ruth married a wealthy man who was compassionate and loved God. She received a wonderful upgrade as the name Boaz means Redeemer and strong pillar. The big news is that Ruth is grafted into the lineage of Jesus because her son Obed was King David's grandfather. The favor of God was shown in her life because she chose to serve unselfishly for all the right reasons and trusted God to figure out the details.

GETTING THE CALL

Bzzzzz! Bzzzzz! I glanced down at the vibrating phone as we sat down to eat at a local diner. It was the first time in many days we had even left the hospital to do so. I glanced down to see who was calling. It was our oldest daughter. I was tempted to ignore her call and eat first as it smelled delicious. I had been reluctant to leave Bill at the hospital but he had insisted that he was okay. It had been a long week and I had subsisted mainly on junk food from the vending machines. Every day as I drove by a quaint old fashioned diner on the way to the hospital, I promised myself to eat there just as soon as Bill started feeling better.

Against my better judgment, I picked up the phone.

"Hi, sweetie," I said cheerfully. "You'll never believe where we went to eat!"

"Mom, why are they taking Dad to Intensive Care? I just called to talk to him and the hospital said that he has been transferred to ICU," my daughter replied.

"There has to be some mistake. I just left him less than thirty minutes ago. He was fine," I insisted.

My sister-in-love, who was with me, paid the bill and got our food to go while I went out to the car to compose myself. I laid my head on the steering wheel and cried, "Oh God, how much more are we going to have to go through?" Fear gripped my heart. Why was my wonderful husband going through this? What would I do if I couldn't take care of him? What if he died?

On the short drive back to the hospital, I cried out to God for strength and courage. This is the emotional ride down a new set of rapids when your loved one is in the hospital. It was true that he was not getting any better and I feared that he might not survive this treacherous turn for the worse.

It had been a tough week. I had taken Bill to the emergency room because he was severely dehydrated and weak because he could not swallow. It was determined that he needed to have a feeding tube put in his stomach. It was a simple procedure and in theory, he should have been able to go home within a couple of days. However, that didn't happen because every time they put him on the operating table he stopped breathing. They kept giving him breathing treatments that made him feel worse.

When I got to the hospital, I was told that the doctor on call decided that it was time to find out why Bill was getting worse instead of better. They assembled a team of specialists who were going to evaluate his case. We were all ready for answers — especially Bill.

What were you doing when you got "the call?" You know the one where your parent fell, your loved one found out their cancer returned, etc. The details are all very different, yet we all can relate to the internal shift that happened within us where we steeled ourselves to take swift, efficient action because someone we loved needed us. For many, accepting this challenge to become a caregiver was not an option, or at least you felt that way at the time.

In other situations, you may not have gotten a critical call but ended up in the role of caregiver by default. You were the sibling who lived closest to your parents who were getting forgetful. Or, you were the oldest who always seemed to take charge when something needed to happen. Or, perhaps you were the one who was single or who didn't have any children. Regardless of the reason, after that call, you became a caregiver in one capacity or another.

Caregiving is like a journey through the Grand Canyon. Many of us started out thinking it was going to be a short ride. "Surely things will improve quickly and we will all get back to our 'normal' lives." When that does not happen, we can become weary and resentful.

Accepting the Role with Honor

Why are you caring for your loved one? Are you complaining about all you have to do? Are you feeling overwhelmed and telling everyone about it? Does it feel like this season will last forever? Does it feel like you are doing "all the heavy lifting" while others seem to stand on the side lines offering to help but never really doing anything significant? Do you resent the sacrifices you make and wish things could be different?

Don't give the acceptable answers here or what you think others want to hear. Instead, dig deep and search for your motivation. If you are a martyr who is 'stuck' with a burden, you will be in for a hard ride. If, on the other hand, you see this as a relatively short assignment of honor from the Lord, you will reap great rewards, learn valuable lessons, and create a legacy.

Hope Tools

ASK FOR GOD'S PERSPECTIVE

If you are a caregiver, you have a front row seat to see and experience suffering. Why do good people have to suffer? You may feel angry at God and doubt His goodness in Your life. When you have doubt, you can lose faith and hope for the future. The realities you face every day can come crashing down on you, especially if you keep it all inside. It is far better to face what you are feeling and move forward with truth. Here are some things that you can do when you feel anxious:

Quiet your thoughts

When facing a medical emergency, your thoughts can race ahead with the worst possible scenarios just as when I was confronted with Bill's transfer to ICU. Medical professionals want to prepare you for the worst and this can cause your fear to increase and grow. It's important to keep breathing and to focus on what you're feeling. Capture your thoughts and see what you believe. At the root of my anxiety as I sat in the car was the fear that I would not be able to care for my husband or that I could not make it alone if he died.

Face your fears

Once I put words around what I feared most, I could ask God for His perspective in it all. I may know what the Bible says and the answer everyone expects me to give. This intellectual knowledge is not enough to replace the fear. Only perfect love can replace your fear and that love can only come from God. Express what you fear to the Lord and ask Him for perspective. "Lord, I am so scared because I don't think I have what it takes to be

Bill's nurse. I don't know what I'll do if he dies. What do you want me to know?"

Listen carefully

God speaks to us in many ways. It may simply be a thought or a few words that pop into your mind. In my case, I may get a mental picture, which is what happened. I saw a picture of Jesus standing at the head of Bill's bed. The Lord was stroking his head in the same way I used to do it with our children when they were babies.

Feel peace

The days ahead continued to be rough yet I knew the Lord was with us every step of the way. When I felt anxious thoughts as I sat by the hour in the waiting room or when they would let me go into ICU to see my husband, I would reflect on the picture the Lord had shown me and I would have a renewed sense of His presence and care for us in this dark time.

ELIMINATE NEGATIVE ABSOLUTES

You get to choose every day if you will dwell on the negative or seek a positive approach to the challenges you face. Remember that you can choose a positive perspective in every situation. This may be hard to do when you are surrounded by those who have established a thought pattern of negativity. Have you noticed that most negative comments contain words like never and always? Replace these absolutes with phrases such as: "I choose to do _____ joyfully so that I can establish the standard of care that _____ (name of care recipient) needs."

Trust God for a Good Ending

You may not feel this right now but one day you will look back on this time of caregiving with gratitude as a wonderful opportunity to honor. The days ahead will no doubt be challenging but you will make it through this difficult time with greater strength, a legacy of funny stories, and the knowledge that you honored fully. Focus on how the Heavenly Father truly loves all of you. Ask Him for guidance and wisdom to begin to see the fulfillment of His promises to you. You will discover how creative and committed He is to surprising you just when you need it the most. Be alert for the upgrades He is sending you. Keep a journal of the daily victories and consistent steps forward. Make a list of all the rewards you and your family are receiving during this time. Your life is the laboratory of how this hope stuff works and time will tell what amazing outcomes will be for a powerful legacy for the next generation.

Honor Key

When you treat your caregiving assignment as a temporary one, you will be on the lookout for surprising ways to honor.

Prayer

Thank You, Lord, for Your presence even when I don't feel You are here. I recognize that my fear(s) can keep me from sensing Your closeness and care for me when I most need it. I quiet my heart before You and confess my need of You. I bring these anxious thoughts and emotions to You and ask You to replace them with Your love, peace, and hope (2 Corinthians 10:3-5). I cannot manufacture this feeling so I will stop trying so hard to be brave. Instead, I will lean into Your all-sufficiency as I trust You to provide everything that we need.

Restore my hope that I have lost in this intense time. Sometimes it seems so dark that I cannot see the way to keep going. I remain confident that my faith in You will lead to abundant rewards and the fulfillment of every promise (Hebrews 10:35 Voice). It seems like a long, hard road ahead, yet I know that as I remain steadfast You will lift the weariness and provide the vitality that I need to provide quality care (Isaiah 40:29 Voice). I trust You to bring me into greater freedom and joy than I ever thought possible.

I am grateful that as I have compassion on those who are in the prison of dementia or poor health You will provide greater blessings on my life and the lives of my loved ones. With your help, I will not abandon my confidence in You to bring good from these hard times as I keep my heart right before You (Romans 8:28).

In Jesus's name. Amen.

HOPE EXPRESSIONS

Remember this, and do not abandon your confidence, which will lead to rich rewards. Simply endure, for when you have done as God requires of you, you will receive the promise.

Hebrews 10:35–36

Shifting Focus

I spent the first night in ICU with my husband. His diaphragm was no longer working so he was relying on a ventilator to push the air in and out of his lungs. The diaphragm is such a small organ that most of us don't ever think about it unless we are taking singing lessons or working out in some new way. You may not even be aware of how critical this small muscle becomes to your breathing because it is part of the autonomic system that works whether you think about it or not – that is, until it stops working.

Suddenly conscious of my own breathing process, I took in a deep breath and let my diaphragm expel all the air. How simple these actions seem when your body works properly and how helpless you can feel when someone you love is unable to do something that should be automatic!

The rhythmic sound of the ventilator was in 4/4 time. Normally, I would have started composing my own song. I've done that before in dark times of my life, but not tonight. My heart was broken; our future seemed uncertain. Tomorrow they would cut Bill's throat and put in a tracheostomy to allow the air flow to go directly into his lungs. I had just read the long list of risks both during and after the surgery. This was a true game-changer. I couldn't find my voice to sing right now.

Earlier that day I had seen a mental picture of Jesus stroking Bill's head as he lay in the hospital bed. That vision had faded in the reality of what we were facing. All I felt was fear and as I gave in to that feeling it seemed like hopelessness and darkness enveloped me.

My husband finally slept as I squirmed to find a comfortable position in the chair provided for me. I was grateful they let me stay close by. The ventilator's sound continued to establish the rhythm of his breathing. I couldn't sleep, so I focused on the sound. A song popped into my head. It was a worship chorus that put a melody to a wonderful Scripture — Zephaniah 3:17. "The Lord Thy God in the midst of Thee is Mighty. He will save and rejoice over you with joy. He will rest in His love. He will joy over thee with singing."

The Lord was right there in the middle of the mess and the chaos of the ICU. He was the calming force when I had more questions than answers. His love calmed me as I allowed myself to trust Him fully. He was my champion ready to rescue me. Of course, I wanted the rescue to be a certain way. That was the hardest part to release— the expectations of a specific outcome. For now, I chose to rest in the confident assurance that He would continue to provide me everything that I needed just when I needed it the most. There is no room for fear when He shows up. I fell asleep with that song resonating in my heart. I was aware of the Lord's presence with us. And, for now, that was enough.

The next morning, I walked down to the cafeteria for a hot cup of coffee in an attempt to bring warmth to my body. I walked through the lobby with a heavy heart for what could be ahead for us as a family. Before going back upstairs, I walked outside and sat down on a bench outside to watch the sunrise.

It was a cloudy day and hues of pink and orange filled sky. Then it suddenly became ominously dark. I started to go back in as it felt like the darkness was closing in. However, just as the dark clouds seemed to cover the warmth of the sun, a slice of light poked through. I sat there for several minutes and watched this happen over and over again until the entire sky seemed like a canvas with glorious rays going up and down. My heart was comforted for the ride ahead. These were the "hope rays" that God had used to encourage me during other difficult journeys. He was faithfully reminding me that He is constant and He is still there even when things look dark.

Hope Tools

FOCUS ON THE BEAUTY THAT SURROUNDS YOU

When you feel overwhelmed, it is tempting to not allow yourself time for any simple pleasures. Give yourself permission to shift your focus from your responsibilities as a caregiver to the beauty around you. There are so many good things in life. It might be the taste of a cup of hot tea with honey (substitute your favorite beverage). Slow down and savor the feel of the warm liquid and describe the taste. Keep a journal of beauty highlights for the day. Go outside and enjoy the warmth of the sun. Lay down on a blanket and look up at the clouds. Look up at the full harvest moon. Close your eyes and listen to the sound of the wind rustling the leaves of the trees.

ALLOW YOURSELF TO FEEL

When you unexpectedly hit a rough spot, the last thing you want to do is sing. It can seem hopeless as you scramble to remember a medical procedure or make calls about medical bills. The burden becomes great and you feel weak. Resist the temptation to harden your heart so you feel no emotion. Instead, choose to sing. It can be a sad song that makes you cry. That's okay. You don't have to manufacture the joy. Embrace what you are feeling. Tears are your friends. You don't have to hold it all together. Gather up the sadness and offer it up to the Lord. He wants to carry the burden for you. Your part is to begin singing praises as you look up for hope rays.

WRITE YOUR OWN SONGS

You don't have to be a musician to do this. There are rhythms to be found in everyday activities such as the vacuum, wind shield wipers, and the swish of the dishwasher. Find your favorite verse of the day and put a melody to it. If none pops into your head, take a song you already know and put the words from the verse to it. Play your favorite music and sing along. Make a playlist of your loved one's favorite music and sing together.

Take a Deep Breath

One of the main reasons for burnout is the feeling that you have more to do than you can accomplish. It seems like you will never catch up. All the pieces of your life seem to be breaking one by one. When a crisis comes, you go into work mode and function through it. When you are anxious your breathing becomes shallow and you stop getting the life-flowing oxygen your body needs during this crisis. If it seems like you are running too fast to catch your breath, it's time to stop and take a deep one.

Set your timer for ten minutes and lay down on your back. Take a deep breath from your diaphragm; hold it to ten seconds; release it slowly. Continue to do this until your alarm goes off. Let your mind float freely to whatever thoughts are there. Do not stop to analyze them.

Your heart rate will slow down, the crazy thoughts in your brain will become calmer, and you will begin to feel peace. Once you are finished, take the anxious thoughts to the Lord and let Him give you His perspective.

PRAY FROM GOD'S PERSPECTIVE

Caregivers need to pray from a faith standpoint. Prayer brings hope and light to dark situations when you line up with what God wants for you. The best way to know what God wants for you is to focus on the verses the stand out to you as you read the Bible. When the weariness and the weight of caregiving threaten to cause you to capsize when you hit the rough spots, hold your breath when you go under, keep paddling, and trust that you will get through this.

God's perspective changes everything, so you can now align yourself with who God believes you are. He does not see you as a pathetic victim of your current situation. He sees you as an overcomer and a warrior. Each chapter in this book closes with this type of prayer. Pray them out loud and declare the truth of the honor and beauty you are discovering. You may even need to flip to the end of each chapter and pray all of them. Other times, you can take that verse that stands out as you read the Bible and allow it to come alive. It can become personal as you put names and situations right in the middle of the verses.

Honor Key

Discuss your favorite songs and find ways to sing them together. Record a video for future generations.

Prayer

Thank You, Lord for Your presence that brings me an eternal perspective and sets my heart free to feel so much joy that I can't help but sing. In my darkest hours, You have promised to show up with abounding grace and tender mercy. There is great joy right here in the middle of it all as I pause to take in the beauty that surrounds me. I rejoice in Your strength as the sun comes up every day with a beautiful sunrise because it reminds me of Your loving mercy and new beginnings. You defended me in my most troubled hour and provided the shelter that I needed at just the right time (Psalm 59:16 Voice).

Give me the same joy that You feel as I celebrate before the good has manifested. There are days I desperately need to see Your mighty hand at work so I choose to sing of Your goodness despite what my circumstances look like right now. You bring rest, assurance and peace because of Your great love. I am amazed that You enjoy this relationship as much or more than I do. You sing and dance over me with great love and affection. As I tune into Your joyful song and join in the dance, I can sense Your delight and pleasure (Zephaniah 3:17). Thank You for the grace to cling to these truths as I navigate through difficult waters in this challenging season of caregiving.

In Jesus's name. Amen.

HOPE EXPRESSIONS

The Eternal your God is standing right here among you, and He is the champion who will rescue you. He will joyfully celebrate over you; He will rest in His love for you; He will joyfully sing because of you like a new husband.
Zephaniah 3:17 (Voice)

Adjusting to the New Normal

Caregiving is made up of a series of rapids followed by pools that give you time to adjust to the 'new normal.' My journey with Bill was no different. We spent an entire day in ICU waiting for the recommendations of what they were going to do for him as his diaphragm was not functioning and he could no longer breathe on his own. It was frustrating to sit and wait. He could not talk because the ventilator was doing the breathing for him and he had a mask over his face. He wrote a few notes on a piece of paper and would squeeze my hand. This was such a scary time for both of us as we did not know what was coming next. That night as I was headed home, Bill motioned me over to see what he had written on a piece of paper: "God is healing me. I'm healed."

On the way home, I was thinking about how it had seemed like a wasted day of waiting. It reminded me that hope in Spanish is *esperanza*. It has the connotation of waiting. Most of us lose hope because life's timing does not match our expectations. In your role as a caregiver, it can be easy to beat yourself up for what did not happen in the past. Instead, revive the hope of what you are destined to fulfill in your life. You are so much closer to reaching the end of your trek than you can even imagine. hope wins when you press toward the purpose you've been given. Celebrate today as if it is already happening and know that you're closer than you think.

I rested well that evening with a great sense of peace.

During the last week and half, the hospital had become like a home away from home. As I clicked the button to get access to ICU, I said a prayer for strength for the uncertainties of that day. I walked past several patients who were hooked up to machines and said a quick prayer for each one. When I walked into Bill's room, he was sitting on the side of the bed. The ventilator was turned off.

"Hi gorgeous," he said with a smile.

I ran over and hugged him. I was overjoyed to hear his voice.

We spent the rest of the day with one specialist after the other coming in. The pulmonary specialist sat at the end of the bed and stared at him for a long time. He kept shaking his head in astonishment. Bill just sat there and smiled. They scheduled his surgery for the feeding tube and moved him out of ICU. A few days later, we went home with instructions on how to use the feeding tube.

God heals and sustains. We were given the gift of two and half more years together. They were tough ones in some ways and glorious in others. This was one of the most exhilarating days in our ride through the rapids of caregiving because we saw a tangible miracle of healing in Bill's body. We held on to the miracle of what God did that day and were grateful for every day of life.

After Bill came home from the hospital, there were many adjustments to be made. At first, he did extremely well in feeding himself through the feeding tube. He insisted on doing it himself and even joked about what he was eating that way. In time, his body adjusted to this new way of getting nutrition and he even would sit at the table with us. At that time, he could still talk. It seemed like things couldn't get any worse, yet they did.

About once a quarter, I would have a reality check. Despite my best effort and heart-felt prayers, Bill continued to steadily decline. It was so hard to see this tall, handsome man shrink physically. He never complained and found it very hard to ask for help. It was up to me to see that he needed help and to offer assistance. One of the greatest gifts I gave Bill was to never treat him with the pity you give someone who is handicapped. In that process, however, I became unkind and intolerant. I regret the harsh words I spoke to him when he couldn't keep up with me or expected what I thought "was just too much." I have chosen to let the Lord carry that guilt for me.

WAITING WITH HOPE

Hope can be in short supply when you are waiting for the results of a medical test or for a loved one to be released from the hospital. Psalm 27:14 (Voice) says, "Don't give up. Wait for the Eternal in expectation, and be strong. Again, wait for the Eternal." The Hebrew word here for wait is *kava* and means to bind together as in crafting a rope. It literally means to gather strength to hold on as long as you need to as you are expecting a good result from the Lord. You are not just waiting – you are waiting on the Lord. Therein is the difference. Your waiting can be filled with hope and the expectation of a good outcome. In fact, as you rest, your mind is transformed because you see the hand of the Lord in every circumstance. Delays are good and have a purpose.

As a ray of hope shines into the areas where you are waiting, you find that you have more energy. You find purpose in things that in the past bothered you. A sense of expectancy can replace the dread that engulfed you. This change can happen even before your circumstances change because you are focused on the Lord. Your perspective changes as you see opportunities and potential. You live in such a way that you wake up ready to get going, accomplish what you need to do and still have energy to help others.

REDEFINING SURRENDER

I remember during this difficult season of caring for my husband that we sang a song at church that spoke about the need to 'surrender' to the Lord. I started crying as we went into the chorus that says, "Forever I surrender." I felt anger rise inside because this wonderful man was suffering so much. We prayed every day that God would heal him and had seen healing miracles in our years of ministry. God healed Bill in ICU but now he was gradually getting worse. At that moment, surrender felt like giving up. Have you ever felt that way?

Surrender is such a hard word. It speaks of losing because you are weak. It seems like you are abandoning your hope. It can feel like God is asking you to relinquish your dreams and desires. Surrendering is not giving up when you look at your situation in a different way. The Lord is not out to get you. He is not sitting there waiting to take away what is precious to you. Instead, He is moving in your current situation to do a deep work in everyone's life. Surrender is turning the control over to Someone who can do something about it and knows the beginning from the end. Surrender comes with the intervention of grace in our lives at a level that we no longer control. Surrender is release, trust, and confidence that God has a good plan no matter what it looks like right now.

FINDING CONFIDENCE IN THE LORD

Your hope perspective determines how you interpret your caregiving journey. If you believe that God has a purpose and plan, you will honor that promise in ways that will release peace and joy in the midst of the struggles. Choose to look through the lens of hope because it's powerful! Adjusting to the new normal is embracing the current situation with confidence that the Lord will carry you no matter what is going on. You will need courage to face the unknown rapids that are ahead. Enjoy the goodness of the Lord in the midst of it all. It is so much more than just enduring and suffering like a martyr. It is about believing that God is at work in everything – especially those things that you don't understand. We found joy in taking care of a wonderful man who loved Jesus with all his heart. We were experiencing hope in the middle of this trial.

Hope Tools

LET GO

I needed God's perspective to make it through this difficult situation. I felt so helpless. When I asked the Lord to give me His perspective, I instantly had a mental picture of what was happening. I saw myself trying to carry Bill. I was dragging him as best I could but we were both in so much pain. I let go of Bill and looked up. The Lord showed up and was so much bigger than we were. Bill and I were the size of toddlers. He picked Bill up and took me by the hand. We started walking together. In that moment, letting go was the best option I had. I felt safe and my hope was renewed.

In your situation, what would happen if you relaxed your control? Control is deceptive anyway because, in the end, you do not have any control over others and how they respond. What you do completely control is your response to the situation. This response will be determined by your attitudes and belief system. Choose to make wise decisions on what you control and release the rest.

Suggestions for letting go:

- Make a list of what you need to release
- Offer each item up to the Lord for wisdom and courage to trust Him
- Journal or draw the mental pictures the Lord gives you
- Write affirmations based on Scriptures to encourage the mental process of release

Take Time to Enjoy Each Day

Adjust your schedule to allow some personal time every day. In caring for my husband, I had neglected my daily walks. I was consumed with what was happening inside the walls of the hospital. It's okay to take time away. You are not the one bringing the healing. You need to stay strong to care for the one who is sick. Spend some time doing things you enjoy doing. Go for a walk or go shopping, if that is something you enjoy. Schedule your own time into the equation and refuse to feel guilty.

Suggestions for increasing daily enjoyment:
- Schedule your exercise time every day
- Partner with others who enjoy doing the same things so they can hold you accountable

- Jump on your bed like when you were little or have a pillow fight
- Try a new, healthy recipe

WATCH FAITH GROW

*Faith is being sure of what you hope for,
and certain of what you do not see.*
Hebrews 11:1

Faith means that you believe no matter what happens. Your hope is to see restoration and healing. We saw the manifestation of God's healing power to restore Bill's breathing. Faith grows and expands as you press into the experience of trusting God in every circumstance. That's where hope intertwines with faith so that you can hold on even when you continue to get bad reports from the doctor.

Suggestions for growing faith:

- Download a Bible app that reads scriptures to you and listen to it every day – See Romans 10:17

- Keep a miracle journal where you list the date of the prayer request and the date of the answer
- Share your testimony of victories from the past

LEARN EVERYTHING YOU NEED TO LEARN

Where does hope come from when the ride gets rough? It comes from God who is the true giver of life and hope. Everything changes when you begin to gain His perspective about the hard times you are going through. Resist the temptation to rush through the hard times without learning the valuable lessons contained in each one. Remain passionate and wait for the future with an expectant heart that truly believes that God is good and has your best interests at heart.

Suggestions for learning:

- Keep a chart of your progress of learning how to care for your loved one
- Talk with someone about what you have learned in the last year, six months, month, week
- Make a list of lessons learned and the benefit of each one

HELP OTHERS WHO HAVE LOST HOPE

Once you have faced trials, you no longer avoid eye contact with others who have lost hope. Instead, you listen to them and encourage them to flourish and become stronger in the midst of their trials. It is in that setting that God's love overflows and is so abundant that you can't contain it. It's spilling over abundantly because it's the result of knowing that no matter what you are going through, you are surrounded by others who are willing to open their hearts with love and compassion. Listen patiently to another person who is going through a trying time. This creates a community of transparent hope, overcoming faith, and passionate patience.

Suggestions for helping others:

- Be on the lookout for Hope Opportunities every time you go somewhere
- Keep a journal of how your experience is helping others
- Listen carefully to someone who needs it and repeat back to them what you heard them say

Honor Key

Discuss challenging times your loved one faced when he or she was young. Talk about what they learned and what they want the next generation to know.

Prayer

Thank You, Lord, for the faith and hope that rise every morning along with the sun. This reminds us that Jesus, the Son of righteousness, also rises with healing in His wings. Thank You for healing all those who are suffering today. You are the Healer and we believe You to bring Your touch to every person who needs it today (Malachi 4:2 TLB).

I am thankful for how You are working in my life during hard times. I am grateful for the opportunity to bless my family by serving them (Galatians 6:10 Voice). Grant me the wisdom to recognize when I have lost the expectations of Your goodness during the waiting times. I turn to You and ask for the ability to lay hold of Your perspective for our lives. Thank You for the people You have placed around me that help and support us. I choose to rest in my confidence in You and never feel short-changed because I am keenly aware of Your abundant love and care for me during every turn on this part of our life (Romans 5:5 MSG).

Thank You for continual strength and courage to face each new day as it comes. I am grateful that You have just what I need at the exact time when I need it. As I face the challenges of this current day, I pray for continued reassurance that You are perfecting genuine peace within me. Thank You for guiding me through this difficult ride and for the courage to face the next wave. I am grateful for the promise that You know what's going on and have a purpose. Knowing this, I rest in that confidence and thank You that others can often see the shine more than we can (Psalm 19:13 MSG). I pray You will glorify Your name through my life and receive all praise and honor.

In Jesus's name. Amen.

HOPE EXPRESSIONS

But for you who fear my name, the Sun of Righteousness will rise with healing in His wings. And you will go free, leaping with joy like calves let out to pasture.
Malachi 4:2 (TLB)

Asking for Help

Recently, I spoke with a friend who needed to vent as she is caring for her mother-in-law. It sounded something like this:

"I just can't believe it!" she said loudly. "We are the ones who care for her day and night. We brought her into our home and wait on her hand and foot. Is there ever any gratitude? What would it hurt her to say thanks occasionally? Then her daughter, who couldn't find time for her when she lived next door to her, is the perfect child just because she sends her little presents on special days."

She continued to unload for a while longer. Finally, she looked up at me with tears in her eyes and said, "Does this ever end?"

When she finally had no more to say, I gently asked, "Need a hug?"

She started to cry and nodded her head. I reached out to her and gave her a long heartfelt hug. I knew how she felt because I have walked through a similar situation in my own family. She sobbed while I hugged her. She finally relaxed and looked up with a big smile on her face. She took a deep breath and said, "I feel better."

Caregiving may start with "the call," yet continue with ongoing crises that must be solved. Each situation erodes your sense of well-being and takes its toll on you. In the chaotic changes that follow, it can be hard to ask for help. Other times when you do ask for help, strained relationships can make it hard for other family members to respond.

Do you sometimes wonder about all the great things you could do if you were not carrying the heavy load of caregiving? It can be easy to get discouraged and feel overwhelmed with the burden of responsibilities. It seems like no one notices all that you do. It's especially hard when you receive no tangible expressions of gratitude from those you take care of and others don't seem willing to carry their weight.

As I look back on this season where my husband needed full-time care, I realize that it became easy to become the indispensable caregiver — the one on whom he depended for everything. I wore my super-duper-caregiver cape well. This was in part because my husband was a very private individual and never wanted to be a burden on others. His servant heart reached out toward those who were helping him more than focusing on his own needs.

I was laid off from my job two months after my husband's long hospital stay. The severance check and our savings allowed me the privilege of being able to care for him. Just when we were starting to run out of funds, one of my clients called with an offer for some work in another state. It was time to ask for help. We called a family meeting to divide up the caregiving responsibilities. Our children bravely stepped up to do a marvelous job of caring for their father. It fell to me to write down everything I did for him. What had become routine for me needed to be written down so they could easily follow the routines we had established for his care. I was amazed at how long the list became, such as add his vitamins and medication to his liquid food, feed him through the feeding tube, empty the suction machine's bowl, and more. There was a lot in my head that I had not put to paper.

My daughter told me that the first night that she came to the house to get her dad ready for bed she was shocked at how much care he needed just to get in bed. She sat in her car and just bawled. While it is normal to want to shelter others from pain, this level of caregiving at this precise time was a privilege for our family.

If everyone is telling you how amazing you are in your current difficult circumstances, you may be trying too hard to do it all yourself. There are just some things you can't fix. Take a deep breath and release the need to make sure everyone is okay. Be honest about what you are feeling and let others do the same. Ask others to step in so they can get the same blessings promised to those who honor.

Hope Tools

HAVE A FAMILY MEETING

Everyone should be present – no exceptions. If those who live far away are unable to attend in person, you can always use technology so they can be a part of the meeting. Explain recent developments that require their help.

Remember that they are not involved in the daily routine and may not realize that the situation has changed. Be sure to allow time for them to ask questions. Lay down all defensiveness to educate them on the need and give them opportunity to respond.

Stop being so strong and heroic. Take off your super-caregiver cape. Prepare a list of specific ways that others can help ahead of time. This is not the time to make others feel guilty. Do your best to remember all the times they have asked for ways to help you. Remember that you said that you had it all handled. Let them know how they can help financially. Let people step up to what they want to volunteer to do or have the capacity to do.

When someone says, "What can I do to help?" take them up on their offer. Pull out the original list and give them several options. Stop being afraid to bother others or to put them out. Don't apologize for needing their help. Train others to know what to do when you step away for a few days. They will be thrilled to help and it will give them special time with your loved one.

SET REALISTIC STANDARDS

This is not a time to be a perfectionist. Write down all procedures needed so that you will have the 'manual' you need. It is important to make this notebook before you need it. There will be certain procedures that must be done in a certain way but others that can be more flexible. Make the instructions as clear as possible to make a smooth transition. Let others read what you have written to see if it is clear to them as well. Let them practice and demonstrate that they are comfortable doing what needs to be done. When I got back home and resumed my caregiving duties, my husband expressed his gratitude for all I did but expressed that he missed my daughter's methodical approach. I think that's because they are so much alike.

Add a tab to this notebook where you can put all the invoices for medical care. This is especially important after a hospital visit as there may be discrepancies that amount to a great deal of money. Keep all the paperwork in one place so you don't have to spend a great deal of time searching for it.

SET AND RECORD ROUTINES

All it takes is one 911 call for you to see the value of organization and having all that you will need in one place. These items will not vary: identification card, medical card, medications, and special instructions. Keep these items in one place where you can find them easily. I kept everything in a small basket in the kitchen cabinet and it was handy any time I needed it.

Establish a written schedule of what you do automatically so you can see how others can help. Make it easy for someone to come in and give you welcome relief. You can go enjoy yourself knowing that your loved one is well cared for.

FIND YOUR PERFECT FIT

Come to Me, all who are weary and burdened, and I will give you rest. Put My yoke upon your shoulders — it might appear heavy at first, but it is perfectly fitted to your curves. Matthew 11:28 (Voice)

Every caregiver needs this verse. There are times when you feel exhausted. Come to Jesus when you are weary. He knows all about what you are going through. Rest as you press in to His love and acceptance. This burden might appear heavy at first but nothing takes Him by surprise. What seems heavy at first can become lighter as you share the weight of responsibilities with others. Instead of complaining about how others are not doing their part, give them opportunities to receive the blessings from the Lord that come through honoring service.

HONOR KEY

Keep a current list of ways to serve in order to allow others to receive the rewards attached to honor.

PRAYER

Lord, You tell me that You will care for me in the same way that a mother cares for her child. What a wonderful picture to have when I am weary and anxious and need a safe place to rest. Open my eyes to see the many ways that You are providing this comfort and joy. I am thankful that I don't have to make it through hard times alone (Isaiah 66:13). You are always close to me when I cry and You send others to comfort me as well. Thank You for all those who surround me that encourage and are willing to help. It is so special because I can receive it as straight from Your heart to mine.

I choose to throw all my worries in Your direction because I know You never intended me to carry them (1 Peter 5:7 ISV). I make a conscious choice to turn all the details of this illness, the financial difficulties, the ever-changing dynamics of our family, and all that concerns us over to You. As I do this, I can stand firm without being shaken (Psalm 55:22). I am grateful for Your concern for me and that You will give me exactly what I need.

In Jesus's name. Amen.

HOPE EXPRESSIONS

But You, Eternal One, wrap around me like an impenetrable shield. You give me glory and lift my eyes up to the Heavens.

Psalm 3:3 (Voice)

Becoming an Advocate

One of my husband's most endearing qualities was that he never complained. Bill was selfless and giving to others to his own neglect. When he started having trouble swallowing, we went to quite a few different doctors. He started swallowing therapy and although he diligently did his exercises, he was not improving. After what would become his last session, his therapist strongly urged me to take him immediately to the Emergency Room.

We were in the waiting area for a long time before they finally took him back. This was in part because I still was very careful about adopting my husband's approach to issues — always minimize the situation and patiently wait. In this case, the problem was that my husband was severely dehydrated. Once they put him on an IV, he felt a lot better. Since it was the weekend, they wanted to send him home. When the nurse came in with his release papers, I requested to speak directly to the doctor. I had not been with Bill when he first said why he was there and felt they needed the whole history of his last meal and how he could no longer drink any liquids. I discovered a new role as a caretaker — an advocate. He needed someone to speak up for him.

In my heart, I knew that if we went home we would be back before the weekend was over and would have to endure another long wait. "Doctor, I respectfully submit that Bill needs to go into the hospital so we can solve the swallowing problems for him to get the nourishment he needs," I said firmly. The doctor looked up with a surprised look on his face because, up to this point, I had been soft spoken and we had even laughed together. I checked in my journal for the dates and other information that could help him make an informed decision. My calm approach allowed the doctor to reassess his first decision and they admitted my husband to the hospital.

Becoming a Hope Ambassador

There were many other times in the next two years where I would need to be the spokesperson for my husband especially once he could no longer speak. I never knew the impact that this had until after my husband moved to Heaven. I called to tell Dr. Goldstein, his internist, about what had happened to him. I got a call back from his nurse telling me how sorry they were for my loss.

"Mrs. Sebastian, you probably were not aware of this but everyone in the office talked about the two of you every time you came in for an appointment," she said.

"I'm not sure what you mean," I answered hesitantly.

"You two were so much in love and there was such sweet unity between you. You are an example of how couples could maintain hope even in the worst of circumstances. We will miss you because this positive behavior is so rare. Please know that your approach to your husband's challenges made a significant difference in our office. I was never able to tell you before but it was clear that you also loved the Lord and trusted Him with your whole hearts. May God bless you and comfort you," she concluded with a break in her voice.

I was in tears as I got off that phone call. I was so grateful that I could be a worthy advocate and a strong Hope Ambassador in the dark times we faced together.

We had found ways to laugh and celebrate the little things and the people who served us. We were able to be a light in dark places where someone needed to be encouraged.

Hope Tools

One of the important roles you play as a caregiver is to be an advocate for your loved one. The medical system is complicated and has many twists and turns. You will have many opportunities to become impatient, angry, and rude. Overburdened medical caregivers may even start the fight. If you choose to win it, you and your loved one may lose in the end. Maintaining honor on both sides of the conversation can make a huge difference.

Below you will find practical tips to enhance your role as an advocate.

REMAIN CALM

It is tempting to get angry when you feel that your loved one is not getting the attention and treatment you think he or she needs to receive. Usually this anger is masking fear. The problem with anger is that it clouds your judgment and may produce the opposite effect from what you were seeking. What can calm you is to switch to the left-brain mode. An excellent way to do this is to take a deep breath, get out a piece of paper, and summarize the desired results. What is the bottom line? What are the specific changes you want to see happen? Partner with the ones who are falling short in that area. Many healthcare professionals are very professional yet may not be warm on a personal level. Keep communication channels open and remain cooperative.

Remember your Manners

You may not know the rules of the establishment. Honor the role of the gatekeepers who are not making the rules but rather enforcing them. Take a step back and look at the issue from their point of view. Never mind that they take such delight in enforcing these rules down to the detail level that it can make you crazy. 'Please' and 'thank you' go a long way in greasing the system, especially if you want to 'bend' the written and unwritten rules in some way or another.

Ask for Clarification

A good script may sound like this: "May I respect-fully ask for more information on why it would not be possible to _____." I learned that the patient has many more rights than they realize. Honor those who are simply doing their job by doing your best to see things from their perspective. The goal is to move in the direction that is best for the patient. Become an avid reader of the fine print. Learn the vocab-ulary. Acknowledge that you could be wrong and simply want more information.

Replace Complaints with Gratitude

Make sure you have a legitimate complaint before you bring it up. There are those times when something needs to be corrected. It is best to respond rather than react to the situation. Start with a compliment and grat-itude for what the staff does or has done for you. Make sure you are talking to the decision maker in the matter as well. It does no good to vent to the answering service who is taking calls on the weekend or evening. Ask for guidance as to the best way to address legitimate issues.

They will be glad you brought it up and you will maintain a vital relationship.

FIND CREATIVE EXPRESSIONS OF GRATITUDE

The way you treat the staff will have a direct correlation to the way your loved one gets treated. That may not seem fair but simply is the way life works. Look for creative ways to express your gratitude to the medical staff who cares for your loved one. This can be a batch of homemade cookies on special holidays or as simple as a thank you card. Find out what kind of food they like and bring healthy snacks like a fruit and cheese tray. You can also provide muffins, soup, or spiced nuts. If they have had to work on a holiday, consider getting them a gift certificate to a grocery delivery service.

HONOR KEY

Look for creative ways to thank and honor the health care professionals who serve your loved one(s).

PRAYER

Dear Lord, thank You that in the rough ride of caregiving You give me everything that I need to move forward with Your plans for _____ (name of care recipient). None of this takes You by surprise and I thank You for Your abundant provision in every area of need (Philippians 4:19). I release all control over the difficult situations we have faced recently.

As I become an advocate for _____ (name of care recipient), may it reflect Your grace and mercy toward all those who work so hard to care for my loved one. Thank You for these wonderful health care professionals who are guiding us during this difficult season. Strengthen them as we partner together to see the best outcome possible. I am grateful that I can remain at peace (Isaiah 26:3 Voice) no matter what chaos is circling all around me. I trust You when I don't know what is going to happen next because You do know and will work everything for good (Romans 8:28).

I trust that You give us life and support that life down to our very breath. I love how You keep my heart safe as I trust in Your goodness even amid these medical emergencies. Sometimes it feels like You have a strange way of showing Your delight in me, yet what You have produced in me during these trying times is stamina, strength, and confidence in Your goodness. You do take joy in us — not in our performance, but in who we are and who we are becoming (Psalm 18:19 Voice). Continue to give us joy in You.

In Jesus's name. Amen.

HOPE EXPRESSIONS

How great is the goodness you have stored up for those who fear you. You lavish it on those who come to you for protection, blessing them before the watching world. You hide them in the shelter of your presence, safe from those who conspire against them. You shelter them in your presence, far from accusing tongues.
Psalm 31:19-20 (NLT)

Caring for the Caregiver

My heart was heavy. When I got up in the middle of the night to use the restroom I happened to glance in the mirror. The bloodshot eyes that stared back at me were filled with sadness and despair. I felt so helpless as I saw my precious husband struggling with the effects of Muscular Dystrophy. His diaphragm had stopped working so a ventilator was doing the breathing for him. He could no longer swallow so I had learned to feed him through a tube in his stomach. He used a suction apparatus to suction out his saliva. On a bad day, it seemed like that was all that he did.

How do you keep going when it seems like all you do is take care of the needs of others? How do you find the strength to continue cleaning up messes and dumping urine and saliva? How do you navigate the maze of doctor appointments and medical bills? The person you are caring for no longer can handle the pressure, so you keep it to yourself and carry that burden as well. At some point, there is a shift in the way you relate to him or her.

I was exhausted. I was discouraged. I didn't know what the future held for us and it scared me. I had lost hope.

There is no exhaustion quite like it. I thought I was tired when my kids were babies. This was different. This was a deep, depleted feeling that overcame my entire body. It was partly because of lack of sleep but I've been sleep-deprived before. I was wearing many others hats as a wife, mother, minister, and employee. Besides, I never planned on taking this job as a caregiver—it just happened gradually, over time, as I kept taking the path of least resistance. I took on more and more, and no one seemed to notice.

There were times when I hit the water and felt like I just could not go on. I call it "caregiver fog." Simple tasks seemed overwhelming and I would cry for no reason. The next minute I would lash out in unreasonable anger only to burst into tears again because I felt frustrated and stuck. It was like I was on a never-ending ride down an unpredictable river with white-water rapids. Does this describe you right now? You are not alone in feeling this way. Caregiving burnout is very real because you can easily neglect yourself while caring for others. It is imperative that you secure your life vest and wear it all the time.

TAKE GOOD CARE OF YOURSELF

With all the myriad of responsibilities you face every day, it can be easy to neglect the most important one in the equation — yourself. The message you listen to as your airplane is taking off comes to mind here. It goes something like this: "If there is a sudden drop in cabin pressure a mask will drop down. If you are traveling with a child, be sure to put on your own oxygen mask and then put it on your child." It is crucial that you honor yourself and put your needs first. Even though we know this principle is true, when pressure mounts and something should give, caregivers put the oxygen on others first. After a while, they find themselves too exhausted to take time to care for themselves. A Stanford study shows that 40% of those caring for a loved one with dementia or Alzheimer's die before the patient. The needs of others can wait while you gain strength and build up your stamina. You need to stay healthy — physically, emotionally and spiritually. Stick to your decision to make healthy changes in your own life. Have you ever thought about what will happen to the patient if you get sick or die?

Hope Tools

SIGNS OF BURNOUT

Caregiving burnout is real and dangerous because it happens gradually. Here are some warning signs:

You experience emotional ups and downs

You are crying one minute and biting people's heads off the next. At one point or another, most caregivers must face the collision of emotional and physical exhaustion resulting from their responsibilities. If you're not careful you can get caught in destructive cycles such as – one day you can't eat at all and the next you can't stop eating. Your brain feels like mush and you no longer care about the things that used to bring you joy.

I do regret snapping at Bill, especially when helping him go to bed each night. He was unable to do this on his own. I would often sit down to watch a favorite television program with him only to fall fast asleep on the couch. He would then have to wake me up so I could help him get to bed. I was cross and spoke angrily. Many nights I would lie in bed asking the Lord to help me with these outbursts of anger, yet repeated it consistently due to sheer exhaustion.

Embrace all that you are feeling. Life has brought you hardships you would rather not face, yet here you are. Admit the anger you feel. Determine whom that anger is directed toward and why you feel that way. Ask yourself if there is any reason to hold on to the anger? Do you feel it's helping you in some way? Ask God for His perspective and let Him carry the anger. I was angry at myself for my responses to Bill when I was exhausted at night time.

It's normal to feel sadness and grief for what you have lost and what your loved one is suffering. Admit your sorrow and release it. The Lord is an expert in carrying every bit of sadness that we give Him. Embracing the tears and shedding them with no shame strengthens you for the days ahead. In some ways, it is what's called pre-emptive grief – mourning that takes place gradually as a loved one's physical condition gradually worsens. (For more details on working through grief, please read *The Power of Hope in Mourning: Ride the Waves to Comfort*).

You are sick a lot and can't seem to shake it

Stress not only affects your emotions, it also lowers your immune system and the ability to fend off sniffles, coughs, the flu, and all kind of infections. While it may not be possible to lower the stress now, you can listen to what your body is trying to tell you and take better care of yourself.

Make it your goal to bolster your immune system with proper rest, nutrition, and exercise. Listen to your body and take care of yourself. Make time for doctor's appointments, annual checkups, screenings, immunizations, and massages. Visit your dentist regularly. Eat nutritious meals, take vitamins, and get the amount of sleep your body needs on a regular basis.

You can't sleep even though you're exhausted

You keep falling asleep all day long. In fact, when you sit still for any length of time, your eyes close. Yet, when you put your head on the pillow at night, you are wide awake. Your body wants to rest but your mind just won't stop. This is a common problem for caregivers.

Set a regular routine to prepare to go to bed and follow it consistently. It is also a good idea not to keep electronics in the bedroom. Avoid late night television because the effects of the screen can hinder sleep patterns. Get as much natural daylight as you can each day to reset the level of sleep hormones. Exercise regularly. This will help you relax which, in turn, helps you go to sleep. Keep a notebook next to your bed so you can quickly jot down the worries that awakened you during the night. If you are still awake, grab this book and begin to pray the prayers at the end of each chapter. Release your worries to the Lord. You will be amazed at how quickly you can go back to sleep.

You feel so overwhelmed that you can't do anything

One of the main reasons for burnout is the feeling that you have more to do than you can ever accomplish. It seems like you will never catch up. All the pieces of your life seem to be breaking one by one. You can't do it all. Your life has changed and many of the things that you have done in the past are going to need to be set aside. In the past, you may have found it hard to ask for help and you even may have turned down help when it was offered. Surround yourself with others who can support you. Open the door to let them help you.

You have been very busy taking care of someone else. It is time to turn the focus toward doing something for yourself. If you are running on empty, take time to rest and even to get away for a few days. Others can pick up the responsibilities that you fulfill. Gain a new perspective and grow as a person. You will return refreshed and ready to go.

Make a list of people that you can call on when you need help. They can be relatives, friends, or neighbors. The important part is to create a safety net and to make it wide enough so that the work load is evenly distributed. Communicate fully that you can no longer do certain things that you've done in the past. Make a list of ways that people can help you and the next time they offer to help, take them up on the offer and ask for specific help. There are also online and local support groups for specific diseases and for caregivers in general. There are many places you can get help if you will ask for it.

You don't make time to exercise

Exercise used to be part of your daily routine. You would get up and go work out at the gym or health club.

Since you have been operating in crisis mode day in and day out, you no longer feel you have the time or energy to follow that routine. Your caregiving assignment has become a marathon rather than a sprint. It is time to shift your thinking to adding daily exercise back to your routine to reduce tension and keep your immune system strong.

Start moving and have fun while you do it. Start small and take a brisk 15-minute walk around your neighborhood. From there, increase the time to 30 minutes and go to a local park. Ask a friend to join you and schedule it into your day. Research has proven that consistent exercise will release endorphins that lower your stress and help you to sleep better at night. You will be amazed at the difference in how you feel.

You can't recall the last time you went out for fun

What has happened here is that you have gradually added in more and more taking care of others until you rarely take time to just to do something fun. The motivation is good because you feel such love and loyalty toward the person you support, yet it is unhealthy. Couple that with guilt for the fact that you are so much healthier, and you find it hard to take a break.

Seek the company of friends who will listen to you vent, yet hold you accountable to give it all to the Lord. Resist the temptation to withdraw from people and to become aloof. When people offer to help, gratefully accept their offer. You need to take a break from your caregiving duties. And, for the record, going to the grocery store or running errands doesn't count either. Go visit a close friend overnight or sit in the coffee shop for a few hours and write in your journal.

Take time to replenish your personal well of strength and resilience. One of the greatest gifts I received when I needed it the most was from a dear friend who would stay with my husband every Sunday while I went to church. This time of gathering with my church community allowed me to recharge and be ready to face the next week.

Honor Key

Change the way you refer to your role as a caregiver. You may not be receiving a high salary, yet you deserve respect as you provide high quality of care.

PRAYER

Lord, I come to You. I am tired and overwhelmed. I can't sleep because I have so many problems running around in my thoughts. I thank You for Your promise to give me rest. I gather close to You as we share this yoke of caring for _____ (name of care recipient). At times, the burden feels extremely heavy, yet I know that as I adjust to this calling that I am in the perfect place. I will live with no regrets as I honor my loved ones(s) (Matthew 11:28 Voice).

I receive the promises that You fill me when I'm empty. I sometimes feel very alone in this caregiving journey, yet You promise to always be with me. I thank You for Your presence even when I don't feel it. You extend your favor toward me in such abundant ways. Give me the insight to see all the ways You are caring for me when I need it the most. Thank You for deep rest (Exodus 33:16). I am thankful that You are indeed near to me right now because my heart is heavy. I know that I can't do this on my own. Help me to be so aware of Your presence, Jesus, that the one I care for, who is discouraged right now, will feel You too. You bring comfort to our hearts by simply being here for us. I lean in to Your presence and breathe in peace and hope.

Lord, thank You also for working in my life when I am in a hard place. I am in one right now and ask that You give me the desire to keep going and doing all that I do. I am grateful that You not only give me the ability to be obedient but the desire as well. I want to stop pleasing people and start focusing on pleasing You. I am so happy to be reminded that I will receive renewed strength and energy as I focus on You (Philippians 4:13).

In Jesus's name. Amen.

HOPE EXPRESSIONS

God is energizing you so that you will desire and do what always pleases Him.
Philippians 4:13 (Voice)

Saying Good-bye

We realized it was necessary to put my mother-in-love into a full care facility when she started falling every night when she got up to go to the bathroom. Bill was no longer able to help me lift her when she fell or to take care of her when I was traveling due to his own physical limitations. This was very hard for Bill because he had promised her that he would not put her in an assisted living facility. Once she adjusted to her new residence, she enjoyed the steady companionship of people around her. I went to see her every day and we brought her home for family celebrations whenever possible. We settled into a routine of loving care for her assisted by the professionals at the facility.

It seemed to make a difference in her care that I was there with her every day checking on her well-being. She was put in a local hospital for pneumonia while I was away on a trip. I went to see her that night when I got home. The doctor said that she was improving and could be released the next day. That night we got a call from a hospital nurse letting us know that she was not doing well. We dressed quickly and got to the hospital as quickly as we could. When we got there, she had just died. Her body was still warm and she had a smile on her face. We felt the presence of the Lord and great peace.

Years later, I sat next to my mother's hospital bed in the living room of my parents' small house in a town in Northern California. She was dozing off and on. Every time she woke up she would say, "Did I tell you today that I love you?"

My answer was a simple, "Yes, and tell me again."

It was such a blessing to hear her words of love. She drifted in and out of sleep with the same question about whether she had told me she loved me that day or not. What a sweet way to show short term memory loss! A few short days later, she died in her sleep. I was grateful for the last few loving conversations we shared as she spoke with simplicity and wisdom about serving God fully without ever turning back.

Near the end of my caregiving season with my husband, his childhood friend came to visit him. At the time, we didn't know it would be the last time they would be together. Rick and his wife, Butchie, were life-long friends of ours.

"Tell them about the shelf," Bill wrote on his whiteboard.

I stood up and said, "Follow me back to our bedroom."

As we walked down the hall, I told them that out of his large collections, Bill had selected some items that he wanted them to choose from to take as gifts to remember him by.

Butchie started crying and said, "I can't take anything."

"Well, you better pick something because he will want to know what you picked," I replied.

As they left that afternoon, I followed them out to their car to talk about what had just happened.

"The doctors are very pleased because both his heart and lungs are very strong," I explained. "As long as he doesn't fall or choke, we are good."

They both cried as I spoke to them so confidently that we would have my husband around for a good while longer. They clung to their 'gift' from him and spoke of how much they loved us. Bill moved to Heaven three months later.

CREATING A CULTURE OF HONOR

Looking back on that experience, I can see that while I was unaware of what the future held, we were creating a strong culture of honor in our circle of friends and family. I am grateful that Bill could share that time with our dear friends and that they were able to spend time together. I have a picture of Bill hugging Butchie; they did not need words. Hugs can honor when there are no words. Take advantage of every single opportunity to honor those you love.

There are many highlights of the two and a half years when I served as my husband's full-time caregiver. The top one, however, is that we recognized and celebrated the measure of God's grace in his life in the midst of suffering. His level of disability increased on a consistent basis, yet he was most concerned about others and not about himself. The patriarch of our family taught us an illustrated sermon of how to establish a culture of honor in our family through serving and loving.

When we express our appreciation, it is usually for what others have done for us. When we started the tradition of honoring the members of our family on their birthday, it seemed to be on a relatively superficial level. Our grandsons were little and so on Bill's birthday, they honored their Papa Bill because he picked them up from school every day and took them to play in the nearest fast food restaurant. After they ate their french fries, they got to play on the playground there.

As Bill's physical capacities diminished, we learned to recognize and honor the essence of who he was and the impact it had on each one of us. When he could no longer speak, he wrote his honoring words on his white board. We always read his tribute last and we were usually all in tears by the time I finished reading. He wrote one of them on a paper that now is sitting in a frame on our son's desk. Fortunately, we took pictures of many of these and they continue to be treasures.

SHARING HONORING WORDS

A eulogy provides kind words that help those who are grieving process their loss, but it is too late for the one who died to hear these loving words. When family relationships are strained or when the communication style in the family is not expressive, it can seem uncomfortable for families to honor one another. We also have few role models for this practice. Add to that the increased stress of caregiving and the result can be frustration and angry words that hurt feelings and separate us from one another. Honor, on the other hand, focuses on connecting and repairing damaged relationships.

In our society, honoring is the exception rather than the rule. For that reason, it can be hard to receive honoring words. Sean, our son, decided to ask Bill's friends to send us emails telling us what they most appreciated about his dad. We printed these messages and created a scrapbook for him. He was overwhelmed with the response when we presented it to him at one of our family meetings. Everyone wants to know that they had a significant impact on the lives of others. Bill's unwavering friendship and grace made a huge difference in the lives of many. We simply gave them an avenue to express it.

"Argh!" Bill yelled from the office. It scared me and I ran in there, thinking that something was wrong. Bill was sitting at his desk with tears running down his cheeks as he read his scrapbook.

"It's just too much. I can't believe this," he said with tears in his eyes.

"It's pretty simple, sweetheart," I said with tears of my own. "The love you have given so freely is simply coming back to you. So many appreciate your friendship and unwavering grace. I am grateful you are my husband. I have learned so much from you." The hugs that followed spoke far more eloquently than any words could express.

LIVING WITHOUT REGRET

Your caregiving situation provides an excellent opportunity to honor. The ideal ride through caregiving is where everyone honors one another and freely expresses themselves. Unfortunately, you may be taking care of someone who is angry and seemingly ungrateful for all that you do for them. If you are in this type of dishonoring caregiving situation, you can choose to honor them whether they deserve it or not. The commands in

Scripture to honor our parents do not say anything about whether they lived an exemplary life or not. It is certainly easier to honor those who are appreciative and kind. The reality is that pain and mental loss can bring out the worst in people. (Be sure to check the Hope Tools below to get you started in the right direction.)

SAYING THANKS

Gratitude changes the environment. You can go into a hostile setting and transform it with simple words of thanks. Your honoring words toward those who don't deserve it can reconstruct the foundation of your family gatherings. It can be the beginning of the release of the promise of hope for the next generation. It may be necessary to look at the very things that irritate you and put a different spin on them. Are you caring for a stubborn old man? Honor his determination and strength. Are you feeling that you do everything wrong because your mother-in-love is constantly criticizing all you do? Honor her attention to detail and desire to teach you the right way to do things so you have less work to do. Are you struggling with how to honor? Be grateful for lessons of what not to do in the final days of your life. There is no way you can lose when you make the firm decision to treasure the experience and live with no regrets.

REWRITING THE END OF THE STORY

I have a friend who suffered abuse from her mother and was alienated from her until her step-father died last year. When she went to visit her mother to find out how she could help, she discovered that her mother was in the beginning stages of dementia. She made the bold decision to move her to another state to live with her. The dementia progressed too rapidly for her mother to live with her for long, but she found her a special home where someone could care for her full-time. On her days off, she takes her mother out to eat, to the park, or for a walk around the block. She has chosen to rewrite the end of her story with honor and love. Her description of this process is beautiful:

"Picked up my mom for an outing to the park. Bought her lunch and she is having the time of her life watching the squirrels! I'm getting a play-by-play of their every move in between bouts of laughter. She thought one was going to get in the truck with us. I told her he was probably looking for nuts. She burst into laughter and said, 'Well, he will probably take me away then! I'm just a big ol' nut!' She's a mess and yet so much fun. Hate her dementia, but so grateful we got to rewrite the end of our story. The other day I was thinking back on the pain I experienced a couple of years ago. At the time, I thought I'd never be able to breathe again. Now I realize, with joy, that I was only letting go to open up to receive more. Life's moments can feel devastating at times. We need to only realize that what waits just around the corner might be so big, so wonderful, that we couldn't contain them both at once. Be grateful for change and blessed with hope."

Hope Tools

INITIATE HONORING CONVERSATIONS

Two weeks before my mom moved to Heaven, I sat in the recliner next to her hospital bed that was crowded into her tiny living room. She slept most of the time and while she slept, I went through the contents of an old suitcase that I found in the attic. I asked her questions that I should have asked her years before. She opened her heart and shared more about herself than I had ever imagined. She was so humble that she never told people about being valedictorian at her high school graduation at age 16. She preached twice at her graduation from LIFE Bible College and presented a special honor to Aimee Semple McPherson from her class. I started listing discoveries about her that most people would not know and shared them at her memorial services. I only regret that I didn't ask the questions earlier. Perhaps she would have been hesitant to 'brag' on her accomplishments. I also discovered that Mom and Dad were engaged three months after they met. (Talk about love at first sight!)

"I just want to make sure you let the grandkids know that we didn't get married for over a year after that," she explained. "Plus, we both prayed and knew it was God's will for our lives."

We talked about how God called her to the ministry and how hard it was to leave her family because at the time she was the only one working. We spoke of her conversation with her mother about leaving and how they both knew that God would provide because they were sure it was God's will.

Here are some questions to ask:

- What was the hardest thing you've ever faced in your life?
- What would you do differently?
- What hard things happened in your childhood that the Lord used for His glory?
- What do you wish you had done in your lifetime that you never got to do?
- What were the happiest days of your life?
- What is the most important message you want to tell the next generation?

Choose Honor Every Day

You have a choice to experience an exhilarating ride through the rapids or complain like a martyr as it seems like it will be endless. Hope means that you acknowledge the difficulties and know that God has a plan for it all. He is working in the midst of the difficult times to show you that you can begin to see that difficult person you care for the same way God sees them. As you love them, you are loving Jesus. He says, "Whatever you did to the least of these, so you did to Me" (Matthew 25:40). He is shaping and molding your life to become all that He has destined you to be. The other benefit is that when it is time to say goodbye you will have a list of character qualities to honor that have already been shared with the beloved one who is no longer present on this earth. You will have expressed your gratitude, what they meant to you, and the legacy they have left.

- Write the name of the person and then make a T-square list

- On the left, list the qualities that irritate you

- Find as many reasons you can be grateful for that situation in your life right now and write them next to each negative quality

- Think of those times you have complained about your caregiving situation. Call one of the ones who tried to console you and let them know you have shifted from complaints to gratitude

- Go to the person you listed and tell them how much you appreciate their input into your life. While this may be one of the hardest things to do right now, it will also be the most rewarding. It can transform the rest of your caregiving journey.

RELEASE CREATIVITY

Look for creative ways to express honor. There are many inexpensive ways to honor the ride of their lives. Communicate to others who they truly are by printing a book of pictures. (Check out ShutterFly or your local drug store.) Enlarge and frame a black and white photo. In the mat of the photo write the story behind that picture. Create a slide show and use one of their favorite songs. Have a themed party around a singing group they like or what they love to collect. For example, my husband collected all things Western so we decided to have a Western themed night. It was so much fun and created priceless memories.

If you have had to place your parent in an assisted living situation, it is important to communicate to those caring for them who that person truly is and celebrate what God accomplished through their life. One of my friends found many creative ways to do this for her mother. She enlarged and framed pictures of her mom on her world travels. She created books with pictures of her mother's artistic expressions. She knew her mother loved to give gifts so she would shop the bargain bins to bring many inexpensive items when she would visit. She decorated a basket and placed the items in them. She would accompany her mother as she let the residents and the staff make choices from the items.

Honor Key

Initiate honoring conversations with the one who is nearing death. Let them know what they have taught you and the difference they have made in others' lives.

Prayer

Dear Lord, thank You for being very near to me because I have a heavy heart (Psalm 34:18 ESV). I know that I can't do this on my own. Bring comfort to our hearts as we prepare to say good-bye to _____ (name of care recipient). Allow me to be a Hope Ambassador by simply being there for our family, being available to let them talk and modeling the work of the Holy Spirit who comes alongside to comfort in very individual ways. Encourage me so I can help others through this grueling season (Proverbs 12:25 TLB).

I am grateful for Your faithfulness as I know You will come through for me. In all these long waits and trying circumstances, I remain alert to what You are accomplishing through it all. Grant me the wisdom to look up for future possibilities that currently feel impossible to see. Grant me the courage and strength to speak honoring words (Romans 12:10) and open topics that may be uncomfortable, yet need to be spoken. Thank You that I don't ever have to give up no matter what is going on around me. I know Your will is accomplished through it all because You are faithful. I am grateful for renewed energy so I can wake up with the energy to accomplish what You have called me to do in this season. I am grateful that I can hope and expect Your will to be accomplished even as I wait (Psalm 27:14).

In Jesus's name. Amen.

HOPE EXPRESSIONS

Wait for and hope for and expect the Lord to come through; be strong, courageous, and resolute; be determined and don't give up; and let your inner man be alert and solid. Yes, wait for and hope for and expect the Lord to be faithful.
Psalm 27:14 (Amplified)

Hitting the Reset Button

Caregiving requires a narrow focus that leaves room for little else but staying afloat and navigating through the obstacles and tumultuous rapids. As a result, it can prove difficult to relinquish this role when your loved one transitions to a different level of care or dies. From the outside, it might seem like a welcome relief. The harsh reality is that it is painful and can leave you feeling lost as you grieve the loss of separation and eventually face the finality of death. You think you will be ready because you have navigated through physical and emotional suffering. People want to comfort you by saying things like "they are in a better place" and that "they are no longer suffering." And still, the house and your heart feel empty. There are many details to take care of and lots of people around. But once the dust settles, it can feel like you have a big gaping hole in your life. Not only are you missing your loved one but also the activities that occupied your mind and filled your time. While they were arduous and emotionally draining, you had a focus and a purpose.

The first time I went to the store after Bill's memorial service, I found myself hurrying to get back home to make sure everything was okay. The emptiness of the house engulfed me as I sat in his lift chair and wept. The first trip I took after he moved to Heaven followed the same pattern. While I was away, it almost seemed like he would be there when I returned. During our marriage, I had traveled extensively for business and always looked forward to my return so I could tell him every detail. It was heartbreaking to walk into an empty house and realize he was not there to share the twists, turns, and hope adventures.

Mourning Well

Take time to mourn fully and completely. I dedicated three years to my mourning process after my husband's death. Part of that process for me was to write *The Power of Hope in Mourning: Ride the Waves to Comfort.* Tears became my best friend as I processed what my life would look like without my life partner. It has not been easy, yet it has been rich and fruitful. Before his death, my husband made me promise that I would continue to live. Take some of the extra time that has freed up to dream again about the next chapter of your life.

DISCOVERING YOUR PURPOSE IN LIFE

At some point, you need to hit the reset button of your life. I learned that the time had come for me to honor my own calling and set a new course for my life. This was not a clear-cut process because I have spent most of my adult life supporting others. I had the opportunity to start what some would consider a 'dream job' that seemed perfect for my skill set. It was the most lucrative job I have ever had, yet after six months it ended poorly and I was fired for the first time in my career. I did some long and hard thinking after that event. I realized that despite the income, I was spending all my time implementing someone else's vision.

I returned to the quest to discover my unique purpose in life. What were the things that only I could do? I determined this would be my new filter before making a commitment to do something. The first thing on the list was to spend time with my family and especially my precious grandchildren. I had already paid for an Alaskan cruise to check off two things on my 'bucket list': 1) Go to Alaska - my 50th state and 2) Take my dad with me to fulfill one of my Mom's desires before she moved to Heaven. We had a wonderful time!

I had put off writing my second book, *The Power of Hope in Mourning: Ride the Waves to Comfort*. I decided to finish it as quickly as I could despite the pain that it evoked as I relived hard times. As I finished writing the last chapter, I felt a definite impression that the Lord was pleased with my progress. It was also time to let go and start living again. Writing this passage for the book started the process for me:

"Letting go does not mean that you forget about your loved one. Deep sorrow does not keep their memory alive. The beautiful, wonderful memories will always remain. You can begin a new volume of your life knowing that the past you had with your loved one marked you forever. That dear one made you who you are. The memories you shared will never be erased and can be cherished. You never let go of the person, but you do have to let go of the life you shared."

About a year after Bill's death, I became involved in a long-distance relationship that ended painfully. Falling in love hurts when the person you think you love does not feel the same about you. It felt so good to be needed that I overlooked some important and critical red flags. I discovered that I need to fulfill what I am called to do first and let God worry about my future relationships.

It is time for you to start living your life. Start doing the things that only you can do. Here are some of the questions I have been asking and seeking to answer: Who am I? What should I do with the rest of my life? What's my style – in clothes and decorating? What are the benefits of being alone? How many decisions can you make on your own?

PRACTICING FORGIVENESS

Regrets and disappointments in life can hold us captive. Even as I wrote the revisions on this book, I had to take a hard look at some roots of bitterness over the difficult caregiving season with my mother-in-law. Most of all, I have had to forgive myself for my lack of honor during that season. I have put this cycle of Forgive – Release – Bless into practice repeatedly.

FORGIVING

At the close of a season of caregiving, you may discover that you need to forgive others for what they did or did not do. This can be difficult when others seem unaware of the issues at hand. Forgive them anyway. I find that the Master's words are the best ones here, so we can say, "Father, forgive them because they do not know what they do." I like to reword it like this, "Father, forgive them because they do not know what they missed." There are many complicated reasons why people do not step up to care for their loved one(s) when they are needed the most. Ultimately, they are the ones who experience the regret for not having done so.

RELEASING

It's one thing to forgive and quite another to release the person from all debt in the matter. Let go of the martyr mentality where someone owes you something, and exchange it for a way of releasing all debts owed to you. In Matthew 18: 23-35, Jesus uses a parable to explain this principle. To modernize the story, just picture a man named Joe, who owes his boss, Mr. Major, over two million dollars. He is about to be thrown into prison for the rest of his life and the debt is to be carried over to his family. He throws himself down on the ground, begging for mercy as there is no way he will ever be able to repay this debt in his lifetime. In a surprising twist of events, the boss chooses to forgive him. Joe leaves the office feeling on top of the world. As he's walking down the hall, he happens to run into Sam, a co-worker who owes him a couple hundred of dollars.

"Sam, you better pay up right now!" Joe exclaims.

"Joe, I'm so sorry. I've been meaning to text you with a payment plan. I just had to change departments and I can no longer get overtime. Plus, my wife has been so sick that she had to stop working," he replies as he hangs his head.

"I'm tired of hearing excuses," Joe yells as he reaches out to choke the penitent offender.

"Please, Joe, I beg you to have mercy," Sam answers with a catch in his voice. "I just don't know what my wife will do if I have to go to prison."

Mr. Major's assistant, Jill, had seen the whole exchange and ran into her boss's office to say, "You might want to come look at what Joe just did."

Mr. Major was appalled to see Sam up against the wall while Joe held him there.

"Stop it right now, Joe! How could you show no mercy after the forgiveness you received of your debt? I'm calling security right now to take you away."

How can you not release the debt of others when you stop to think of all that God has done for you in forgiving your sins through the sacrifice of Jesus on the cross? Release the debt of expectations and move forward in new freedom to a new phase of life.

BLESSING

This is the best part of all. Start thinking of all the ways you have changed because of your season as a caregiver. Make a list of reasons you are grateful you could be a caregiver. It has been a blessing for the person you cared for. That is a given. What's often neglected are the areas where you grew and expanded because of the stretching and pressure. On top of the benefits you have received, speak blessings into the lives of everyone involved.

Hope Tools

FIND YOUR FOOTING

The time and energy spent navigating the wild waterways of caregiving can leave you exhausted. It is easy to neglect your health and to not take the time to do what you enjoy. Most of the time you are so busy that there is no room for anything else in your life. Once this season ends, it is time to rest and take some time off to figure out what to do next. Be careful about rushing to volunteer simply to fill the void. Look deeply at your life and identify the cracks. Repair them with prayer and meditation as you reflect on what brings you pleasure and fulfillment.

As you look at where the ride has taken you, look for the miracles and heightened awareness of your giftings that resulted from your river trip. What experiences can you share that energized you and inspired you to keep going? What were the shifts in your priorities and perspective of life? What are the relationships you want to cultivate and grow? What do you have access to right now that brings you joy and fulfillment?

REFRAME YOUR CURRENT SITUATION

Life can change in one second, leaving you wondering what happened. When I got the call that my husband had died in his sleep, I had to adjust to a whole new life. There is sorrow and there is pain. It is important to feel it completely and embrace the changes that come with it. I have the opportunity to see my situation in the way God sees it. I can either feel lonely or free to spend more time seeking God. I can feel either full of despair for the sorrow I feel or I can look for others I can help who are going through similar circumstances. It is my choice to take a step back and see what good can come from what I am living right now.

As you come out of a season of caregiving, having honored your loved one, you can rest assured that the promise attached to this commandment will be fulfilled in your life. After the two and half years as a full-time caregiver for my husband, my financial situation was at times precarious. I want to testify to the faithfulness of the Lord that He provided abundantly and creatively as I focused on honoring His purpose for my life. Through my obedience to ride over some rough places, I became truly rich in what mattered most and have no regrets. That's truly priceless!

REKINDLE YOUR PURPOSE

Reflect on the things that you enjoyed doing as a child. What gifts did you display then that others enjoyed? Revive the gifts, and look for ways that you can start using them again or expand their use. For example, I loved playing the piano when I was a teenager. I wrote songs and loved to sing them. In the cares of life, I have stopped writing songs. It is time for me to revive this gift and start 'singing a new song' every chance I get. Even if nothing ever happens with these songs, they make me happy.

Write down your purpose. Remember how I spoke of doing what only I can do? I have made a list to remind me not to get sidetracked. Not surprisingly, relationships are at the top of the list. Spending time with those who are important to you should be your top priority because that will be your legacy.

REDEFINE YOUR DIRECTION

The time will come when you are ready to move forward. It is important, at that point, that you know where you are headed. Beware of change for its own sake. Change is hard enough, but when you know what chapter you are starting in your life, the perspective shifts to make room for a new season. Timing is of the essence here. Map out a timeline and move forward without fear. Once you set your focus, the details will fall into place and you will begin to reap the reward of favor and blessing for your faithfulness in doing what only you can do for those you love. Celebrate all forward movement and honor all that you have learned in the wild ride.

HONOR KEY

Forgive yourself for any regrets you have in the season of caregiving and realize it is not selfish to now spend time pursuing your own dreams.

PRAYER

Thank You, Lord, for the very fact that You have given me so many wonderful promises. These promises awaken hope within me to know that no matter what I may be going through right now I have the treasure of knowing that there is a wonderful plan in it all. Thank You for changing my perspective about my future. I treasure those verses that are becoming a part of the very fiber of my life. I have found a treasure because I have found You, and what You say comes true (Psalm 119:162). In the difficult days ahead, grant me the wisdom to live like I truly believe this.

I am grateful for the discipline that I have developed during this season. I release all fear of the future as I continue to love those around me. I know I have everything I need at this very moment and will need in the future because You make me powerful and fill me with Your strength and courage (Isaiah 41:10).

I stand amazed to see that these difficult circumstances that I've faced built me up rather than destroyed me. Thank You for joy and abundance even as I chose to trust You in the middle of the mess (John 10:10 Voice). I chose to have a confident expectation of Your deep work within my heart to develop the fruit of the Holy Spirit in my life. I forgive all those who took advantage of me and I will not allow their indifference to steal my joy. They do not own the joy in my life. You and I do. I choose today to speak blessings rather than complaints. I know that my words are important in setting the mood around me so I choose to speak of what You are doing rather than what others are not doing. In it all, I promise to give You the glory and the praise.

In Jesus's name. Amen.

HOPE EXPRESSIONS

The blessing of the Lord makes a person rich,
and He adds no sorrow with it.
Proverbs 10:22 (NLT)

Afterword

"You know what I would like to do one more time?" Dad said one day in our daily phone conversation.

"What, Daddy?" I answered.

"I would like to eat ice cream on the beach in Costa Rica one last time," he stated simply.

One year after my mother's death, I started planning vacations with my Dad. I had read an article that said that planning for a vacation can bring more positive feelings than the actual time away. Based on this information, I treated this request the same way. One year later, my siblings and I took Dad back to Playas del Coco in Guanacaste, Costa Rica – the country where we were raised.

The honoring highlight went beyond eating ice cream. The beach we had been to years ago was now very commercialized and crowded. Instead, we walked a block from our condo to a small cove with boats anchored not far from the shore. Dad used his walker to get to the water's edge and then, flanked by my brother and sister, hesitantly ventured through the waves to the deeper water where he could float. The minute he plunged into the deep blue-green water, he relaxed into his amazing floating formation. It was as if the years dropped off and he was the young missionary who was teaching us to trust the water to hold us up. He raised his hands in praise. Tears ran down our faces as we honored his wish.

One month before, I had spent time with him to discuss a difficult decision. We had respected his independence as he lived alone with the assistance of someone to clean his house and check on him every day. The small town allowed him to continue to drive. Still, he was lonely and spoke of how it may be time to make a change. That was a challenging month as we discussed every avenue of the move. We packed up a few furniture items for his new place and made the transition.

I was driving my sister's car with Dad in the passenger seat.

"Well, Daddy, it's time to say good-bye to the little house now," I said as we prepared to back out of his driveway.

"You know what, pumpkin?" He spoke quietly.

"What, Daddy?" I replied.

"This house really meant a lot more to your mother than it did to me. I am glad to be walking out of here on my own and look forward to what's ahead," he said.

We chose to honor him in very special ways because of the lessons learned in the other caregiving scenarios. Honor always wins. No matter which type of caregiving situation you are in, remember to honor those you care for and to honor yourself as well. The Lord is very aware of your sacrifice and pleased to see your beautiful servant heart. You have invested unselfishly and will reap a great harvest of peace and legacy of grace and honor.

Now, I have found a new love in my life. I met a wonderful widower through mutual friends and we recently got married. We have started a new ride together. Dad was able to pronounce the blessing found in the Hope Expressions listed below at the end of our wedding ceremony. The lessons learned in caring for my loved ones and mourning my first husband's death taught me take every bit of knowledge gained in this challenging adventure and start a new one. We are excited and putting on our life vests to head for the adventure of our lives in the land of the living.

Will you join us?

Hope Expressions

The Eternal One bless and keep you. May He make His face shine upon you and be gracious to you. The Eternal lift up His countenance to look upon you and give you peace.
Numbers 6:24–26 (Voice)

Afterword

KarenSebastian.com

Author | International Speaker | Hope Catalyst
Shining the light of hope into dark places

Karen Sebastian-Wirth believes God brings the light of hope into the darkest hours of our lives. Driven by her personal journey from despair to hope, Karen candidly shares her heart and the adventures of discovering the beauty of 'hope rays' on dark cloudy days. She has experienced first-hand that life may not be easy when you face challenges you never 'signed up for.' It's in these dark places that the light of hope can illuminate the possibilities and bring you into unexpected venues of promise. Her powerful books offer refreshing Biblical perspectives, allowing you to receive and impart God's gift of hope.

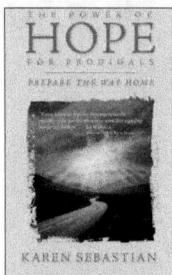

Rather than dealing with issues of rebellion, *The Power of Hope for Prodigals* helps you see your prodigal from God's perspective, enabling you to speak life and experience the transforming power of hope.

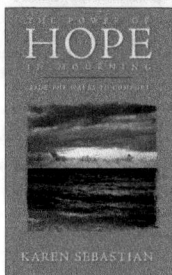

The Power of Hope in Mourning teaches you to 'ride' the waves of grief so that the very pain that threatens to destroy you pushes you into the presence of God where hope and healing await.

The Power of Hope for Caregivers equips you with hope for your challenging role as a caregiver empowering you to serve with honor and complete the journey with no regrets.

Karen Sebastian explains from experience the enormity of the possible when hope seems dim. . . – **Jack W. Hayford**, Pastor/Author/Songwriter

Karen Sebastian-Wirth, who is affectionately known as The Hope Lady, is a dynamic and gifted writer and speaker who shares from the rich experiences of her life. God has given her a transforming hope to not just survive extremely difficult situations, but to overcome and enjoy an abundant life even before the circumstances change.

She will inspire you, teach you, make you laugh and cry as she brings the light of hope found in God's Word, coupled with practical ways to release this energizing power of God in your life. You will love her transparent vulnerability and feel empowered to face life's challenges with courage and hope.

Karen is fluent in Spanish, having grown up as a missionary in Latin America. Her ability to embrace change and train others to do the same has opened opportunities to be a 'Hope Ambassador' both in the church and in the marketplace.

As a caregiver and a widow, she took brave steps forward to fulfill God's calling on her life. She has now remarried and lives with her new husband, Rodney Wirth, in Grand Prairie, Texas, where they actively serve in their church and enjoy their children and grandchildren.

Contact Information: Karen is available for seminars, conferences, retreats and banquets. She travels from Dallas, TX. For more information, please contact Karen at karen@karensebastian.com.

/hopeispowerful   /karensebastian   /hopeispowerful

www.ingramcontent.com/pod-product-compliance
Lightning Source LLC
LaVergne TN
LVHW052027080426
835513LV00018B/2208